THE AMERICAN CIVIL WAR II:

The Fight Isn't about Slavery, but rather, for Our Freedom

T. H. Logwood

T. H. Logwood

" The union must be preserved. This struggle is not over the question of slavery, but rather, keeping the union together. _Lincoln, 1860 Inauguration Address"

WHAT WILL HISTORIANS SAY?

We are headed for War! These are perilous times, and it seems that events are spinning out of control, with conflict as seen inevitable. Are we headed for armed conflict with our fellow citizens? Is another civil war looming? What is at stake is an America that is governed by the Rule of Law, Constitutional law, traditions, and fairness. Or will America sink into a country controlled by "mob rule", a socialistic ideology, where thought and expression are controlled by an elite class that decides what is right and wrong. Such a society of constricting rules would all but destroy our Rights and Freedoms. The battle lines are drawn. What will historians say about this crazy time?

America titters on the brink of war, and the 2020 Presidential Election may well be the spark that ignites the conflict. Although the shooting hasn't yet begun, the pre-election mob violence in the (democrat-run) cities, and the slanderous propagandist media are the precursors. The catalyst may well be the election outcome, similar to the first civil war 160 years ago.

Just look at the news, mob rule and "peaceful" protests are happening in the major cities, the Corona Virus had stymied our otherwise robust economy, mobs destroying historical statues, amidst a turbulent presidential election year. The major controversies these days revolve around defunding the police departments, perceived racism by a white supremacist class, gun control, freedom of speech and religion, and government overstepping its bounds in regards to property and due process. These are just "side shows" to what is really happening. Are these issues real life, or just more emotionally driven hype to push a deeper darker agenda? What will be the match that sets off the powder keg? How will future generations view this time?

These rioting mobs, and leftwing social-warriors are trying to tear down statues, to "right the wrongs of the past". The social justices wackos think that removing or destroying Confederate statues, or those of Washington, Lincoln, Columbus, and others, will change anything, they are chronically deluded. History happened, even the greatest of heroes have flaws and make mistakes, but we are to learn from our past, not cover it up and pretend it never took place. This is just a smoke screen for the larger plan to destroy America, and the rights and freedoms we hold dear.

Are we headed for another civil war? The Leftwing radicals and democrats have been saber rattling about fairness and fascism, at the same time they are threatening to take away rights and force everybody to their will. Hypocrisy and the double-standard are their mantra, while vilifying the president that's fighting for the people.

As history is written by the victors, will the writers be honest enough to talk about the struggle between those upholding our constitutional rights, and those liberal-thinking socialists that sought to change it? Let us de-fuse the sparks of unrest with calm open and honest discussion, and by voting in the next election. Because elections do have consequences.

A Look at the First War

Back in the first half of the 19th century, events were unfolding and developing, to plunge the young United States into armed conflict. The country was still new, a young fledgling nation trying out its radical form of government, the representative democracy, with the notion of individual liberty. The nation had won its independence from the "tyrannical rule" of the English crown, defeated the English again in the War of 1812, while fighting native tribes, and growing at a viral rate. Immigrants were coming into the country with the hopes for a new life under the doctrine of freedom, while others brought in manual labor (namely, slaves from Africa). America, was a land of unfettered opportunity, riches to be had, and a freedom to chart ones own course.

America the young, was not a land of freedom and opportunity for all. The growing numbers of black slaves were traded as cattle or goods, and knew little of the hopes of justice and fairness. The black man was not the only race exploited during this time. Little is talked about the native peoples, who were also made slaves by the encroaching "land-grabbers".

Native children and women were more so the target of the "Red Slave Trade" than the men, but modern historians overlook this tragedy. Treatment of the native peoples has all been whitewashed by most historians, focusing more on the "poor black man", and the terrible plight of the black slaves. From the beginning, perhaps before Plymouth Rock and the Pilgrims, the time of Columbus and the Spanish invasion of the America's, the native peoples have undergone horrible abuses. Wars and slaughter, stealing their ancestral lands, slavery and abuses of every kind, were the treatment of most native tribes. Tribe after tribe were pushed out of their homelands to make way for the new nation. And let us not forget the President Andrew Jackson and his legacy, the "Trail of Tears", the mass eviction of the Cherokee (and other) peoples from their lands. Prejudice and hatred is not solely a black issue, but is certainly a part of our history. It is fair to say, and accurately noted, that people throughout human history have been unkind and often horrible to each other, regardless of skin color.

As the young America grew, and lands were cleared for crops, and the need for labor increased. The black slaves played an integral role for these largely southern agricultural developments. The demand for labor in the northern half of the country was being supplied by foreign immigrants and often children. As states were being added, and the controversy of slave versus non-slave states increased, a divide in the unity of the nation was forming. The premise of moral right and legal rights concerning slavery became a hotly divisive issue. The issues of whether it was right for a nation touting freedom and individual liberty for its citizens to own another human being or not. The argument was countered with the constitutional guarantees of rights to own property, and the non-interference of government in ones daily life. After all, the struggle for independence was about getting the (English) government off their backs. Yet, just a few years after that war, the same issues of control were dissolving the union.

Moving forward a bit, perhaps the spark that started the American Civil War was Rev. John Brown. The pious, yet hypocritical pastor, with his followers, took to armed conflict to force the country to address the black slavery issue. Although there were minor slave uprisings, the struggle for "Bloody Kansas", and other conflicts over the slavery issue, it was the national attention that made the John Brown incident, an exploding powder keg. It was the single-most event that spurred the great bloody conflict known as the American Civil War. To some, it was the "War Between the States", and to many Southerners, it was "The War of Northern Aggression". But however you call it, it was a tragic and horrific period in our history that split the nation apart. It often boiled down to families being torn apart as their loyalties went opposite directions.

Historians debate the causes of the war, but in this modern day of politically correctness, they say the motive was slavery. How sad is that, that the truth gets buried. "History is written by the victors", is a truism, even in this freedom-based America. The truth is, the causes of the civil war is a matter of perspective. It was very much a struggle of ideologies, not unlike the challenges we ace today. Sure, slavery was a major part of it, but if it was possible to inquire of those that actually lived at that time, the truth would be quite different.

For the wealthy, some businessmen, and the southern aristocratic class, as well as a number of politicians, the slave issue was prominently their cause. To the vast majority of average common folk, the conflict was not slavery, but Rights. The average person at that time was poor (or modest) in their lifestyle and income. Their education and perhaps limited understanding of civics and the law, revolved around rights. What a man or government can or can not do (or should not do), is perhaps their simplistic understanding causing the war. Many of the people had gone through, or were children of, the revolutionary war days, and/or the War of 1812. Their understanding of rights and the tyranny of government, was more of a first-hand basis, rather than scholarly theory.

Especially for the southern "rank and file", they took up arms in defense of their homes and families from an invading force (the union army). They were poor farmers and common folks, neither of which owned slaves. You did not get the common southern fighting man to be the zealous formidable soldier he was, by fighting for some rich slave owner. No way, did not happen. The southern cause was about rights and freedom, protecting their homeland (namely their homes and families). But our modern educational bias and political deception indoctrinates our children into the lie that the America civil war was fought over freeing slaves. No, totally false.

And if you study the war, President Lincoln and the north were on the verge of losing. He had stated in his 1860 inaugural address that the conflict was not about slavery, but about keeping the nation together. It was a political maneuver to draw support for the war effort. Only after a major victory (Gettysburg) did Lincoln declare his cause to be about ending slavery, via the Emancipation Declaration. Now understand that this declaration was made only to free the black slaves of the southern states. There were still about 900,000 slaves in the northern states, and it did nothing to address the native peoples that were enslaved.

History books are written and rewritten every few years. For some reason, the notion that all of the books have to be changed every few years, is wasteful of taxpayer money to say the least. The reality is that every new edition of American history whitewashes the truth of what really happened. In this politically correct era of "not offending anyone", or "hurting someone's feelings", history is sterilized and boiled down to broad generalities. The prominent leaders and heroes of American history, like our Founding Fathers are demonized, and the moral values and constitutional ideals are vilified. This "cancel culture" approach to education doesn't change the realities of our history, it just makes our children ignorant, and subject to repeating the same mistakes. History repeats itself, and if we don't learn from our past, the good and the bad, then we are prone to falling into the same blunderous decisions.

Interesting to note, the if one were to discern party politics and the war, it would be said that the republicans and the Lincoln administration were the victors, and the southerners were the democrats. After all, as you study the party affiliations of those in office before, during, and after the war, it was mostly democrats in the south, and republicans in the north. So was the war really between republican and democrat platforms? That is an interesting thought to ponder.

And then today, the rhetoric points to the democrats as the party of unrest, and the republicans as the party of law and order. Again, that is an interesting point to ponder. The republicans stand for law and order, the constitution, a strong economy and armed forces, lower taxes, pro-life, were the proponents of the Civil Rights Movement, and school choice. Whereas the democrats are the ones screaming racism and hate, rule by the mob and a few elites, destroy the economy with regulations and skyrocketing taxes, outsourcing our jobs and manufacturing to other countries, they decimated our armed forces under the Obama/

Biden era, they fight against life, record crime stats in all of the democrat-controlled cities, and insist on government control in all aspects of our lives. Was it not the democrats that controlled the slavery institution, started the KKK, and blocked the Civil Rights Movement of the 1960s? Do the research, check out this supposition.

So what will future historians have to say about these current times? Did we avoid the war?

WE BETTER FIGHT FOR OUR RIGHTS

"Don't tread on me" was a rallying cry during the first revolutionary war. From that world-changing conflict, the establishment of the United States and its governing Constitution came about. And the key part of the constitution is the Bill of Rights, outlining the freedoms that government is suppose to protect and not interfere with. With diligent detail, the Founding Fathers insured that the people would be free from the heavy hand of government controlling every aspect of our lives. The people would be free to speak what they thought, worship as they chose, own property to make their lives better, and have the ability to defend themselves. The document would define how the government would go about protecting the liberties of the people, via a process, and set the boundaries of such liberties as to not interfere with someone else's liberties.

The Constitution is a masterful and powerful document that tried to cover all aspects of government and the people. When great changes are needed, there is a process of "amending" the constitution, and to this date there have been 27 such amendments added. This process is very difficult, not possible to be changed by government alone, but rather through the will of the governed,

However, over the past several decades, our rights and freedoms guaranteed by the constitution are under greater and more aggressive assault. Even more so, over these past few years, there has been many groups and outspoken individuals, plus some of the most radical democrat leaders, are calling for an end to parts of the constitution, and many of our freedoms guaranteed therein. These folks are referred to as "leftists", "socialists", "anarchists", and "liberals". To be fair, not all of them are allied or part of the democrat party, but without question, many of these people are staunch left-wing democrat party leaders and activists. It is those who oppose the Constitution, the Rule of Law, rights and freedoms of the individual, and calling for overthrowing everything normal and decent.

These radicals call for democratic rule versus our representative democracy that has been a check on the consolidation of power. They seek the popular vote instead of the electoral college system that assures a more fair representation of the peoples will. And the latest clamoring is to "stack" the Supreme Court with more justices, whereby the justices would rule based on popularism and politics instead of adhering to constitutional law. And with a controlled court, they can abolish every right and freedom otherwise guaranteed. And the scary part is that during this election cycle, the democrats are very vocal about the changes they want to make.

THE WAR

But how would the war play out? In a war or battle, you typically know who is who, but not so this time. Who is the enemy and what do they look like? What events or crisis moments would be needed for the lead to start flying?

Difficult to say this time, as everything in a traditionally normal war has changed. Like the first civil war, this conflict would also be brother against brother, fellow countrymen against each other. The lines are very blurry and there is no clear way to discern the "good guys" from the "bad guys". It is a matter of perspective for sure.

The second civil war, hopefully will never become a real life conflict. We hope and pray that the ideologies of the liberal socialists, and the constitutional conservatives never plays out beyond the ballot box. But quite importantly, we are in a state of heated tensions amongst our countrymen over ideas. You might actually say, that the war is a war of ideologies, left-wing lunacy versus rational thinking.

Because to many Americans, the ideas promoted by the (fake) news media, Hollywood elitists, outspoken democrat politicians and candidates, many from academia, and radical groups, is total insanity. These leftwing socialist progressives, shout about defunding police departments, racism and "white supremacy", erasing history by destroying statues and monuments, and rewriting history to demonize western civilization and the Caucasian male, saving the planet by eliminating fossil fuels, free schooling and health care, free "this and that", "tax the rich, until there are rich no more", seize our guns, open the borders to the worlds masses, government dependency, and so on. To hopefully most people over the age of ten, these ideas are sheer "stupidness". But it has been a growing trend over the past several decades, where social justice and "equality or fairness", demands harsh measures to right the wrongs of society, even to the point of force and violence to achieve their ends. These are the enemies of the second civil war. They are the socialists, and haters of America, and everything it stands for and has achieved. These are the ones that clamor about President Trump as a fascist dictator like Hitler, yet make demands to follow them or face the consequences. We recognize that history happened, you can't change that, and to try and erase it, is like sticking your head in the sand. Pretty childish.

The defenders or patriots of the struggle, are the average citizen, the middle class, who stand for life, liberty, and the pursuit of happiness, as inscribed in our founding document, the Constitution. The "good guys" are those who stand for peace, upholding the rule of law, justice, the Bill of Rights, the right-wing conservatives, most republicans and independents, just trying to get through life.

Our country became great because of bold leaders and common folks seeking freedom and risking everything to build upon the ideas of personal liberty, hard work, faith, individualism and perseverance. Not that there hasn't been injustices or wrong actions, but as people we are flawed, and "stuff happens". But it is upon reflection and repentance of the past, and trying to "do better" that we have been able to grow forward and become what we are today. Yes, there continues to be wrongs that can be made right today, but there is a process to do so, and it starts with the ballot box. Not with violence or lawlessness, but with calm and open discussion, debate, and selecting leaders that will work for the common good of the people. It is to this normalcy of life that we are called the "good guys" in this war.

Who will the armed forces stand behind? Our current service people, who will they side with? Their Commander-in-Chief is the President, but they have sworn an allegiance to upholding and defending the Constitution ("against all enemies, foreign and domestic"). The same is true with all public servants, from the federal level, all the way down to the local dog catcher, their oath is to the Constitution. How can it be that many in public office display a disloyalty and disrespect to their oath, and spout sedition? Ask the voter.

There are many rich and famous people in this country that made their wealth and positions of prominence from the very ideals they now oppose. The Hollywood jet-set crowd, the tenured professor, the loud-mouth news media folks, the gifted athlete, and the rich businessmen, who now shout for revolution, are the liars and hypocrites that are pushing us into conflict. They got where they are today from the support of the common person going to the movies or sports events, attending the expensive campuses, buying the trinkets, all part of the normalcy of Americana. Now they have turned to the "dark side"? Why? These fools think that socialistic ideals will make them more popular or wealthy? Growing up, I remember the adage, "Don't bite the hand that feeds you".

The war, the battles, what and how, where? That's difficult to know, but it seems that the zombie mobs in the big cities is where the focal point of conflict might take place. With the recent riots across the country, the police have been held back, but what if they weren't? What if the violent criminals were arrested, would more than rocks and insults fly? If you ever watched any movie ever, you would know that the big cities are always a disaster. Armed or violent conflict would likely take place firstly and most intensely in the cities. Throughout most of rural America, the patriots are armed and trained, but the city-dwellers are mostly pacified.

Certainly with inner city violence, warlords and gangs would mark out territory and defend it. Any conflict in the cities would be a fierce guerilla insurgency that would make Iraq look like a girl scout picnic. The tragedy would be the elderly, the children, and the innocents trying to survive (as they currently are). Starvation, disease, and all sorts of depravity would quickly occur, and the inner cities become total anarchy and chaos. Is that any different from right now in the inner cities? Gang warfare, violence, the mayhem, yet the local politicians sit comfortably in their mansions awaiting their next reelection. It's tragic that these leftwing politicians have been in office, often for decades, but never resolving the problems of the real-life struggles of the people.

And at the same time, the media spews out propaganda, and the campuses indoctrinate new ranks of zombies to fill the ballot boxes of the left. This is a war of the mind, teach and preach a doctrine of lies, how socialistic principles will solve the ills of society, and all you have to do is "follow". Elect progressive leaders to write laws that will give you everything (at the cost of everyone else). Write laws to restrict the rights and freedoms otherwise guaranteed, and use the purse to enforce them. Add to the ranks of foreign mercenaries (illegals), that will follow "lock-step" with their leaders.

Like the Revolutionary War two hundred plus years ago, or the first civil war, it took a while before the patriots in the rural areas to "wake up" and take their stand in the fight. And "wake up America" is greatly appropriate today as our liberties are being trodden and threatened. It is time to choose a side, the leftist socialistic insanity, or normal decency and liberty. Fight this fight in debate, and with your vote, before the war begins.

What are the events or "powder kegs" that might set off a real conflict? Rights. If more of our rights, freedoms, and liberties are legislated away, might that be the spark to start the Second Civil

T. H. LOGWOOD

War?

VOTER FRAUD -
THE LIKELY SPARK
OF THE WAR

Back in the late 1850s when the slavery debate peaked, and the radical Reverend John Brown was causing havoc and violence, the country was on the edge of exploding into the feared civil conflict. Right after the failed attempt by Brown and his followers to seize the arms in the Harper's Ferry station, the final straw before the conflict was finally cast. Soon, the nation was at its most horrific point, a civil war.

A little differently than way back then, the issues and situation is greatly different, but the sparks to rip this country apart does exist today. With the 2020 presidential election, just a short time away, tensions are high, and the nation is divided between the patriots wanting normalcy and law and order, versus the radical leftists and anarchists seeking to tear down the status quo. Perhaps the final straw to cast is the controversial issue of mail-in ballots. The democrats, under the directive of Nancy Pelosi, Speaker of the House, have pushed for disseminating some 80 million unsolicited mail-in ballots, that are primed bullets for voter fraud. With crafty intentions, these unverified ballots can sway the election, subverting the true intent of the electorate.

"The only way democrats can win, is to cheat", is something that gets repeated often around election time. Perhaps it's true, perhaps it's overstated, but the fact it that fraud does happen. How much of the actual election or vote tallies are manipulated due to foul play? That is an unknown, although some people have tried to assess the depth and breadth of the problem. The fact is, that in our free and open nation, the temptation to cheat is strong. After all, we are just human, imperfect, sinful, and we will mess up sometimes. And sometimes, the leaders we elect to office, are in fact not the best choices. For some, it is the lure of power, riches, and influence, that can corrupt the soul, and can damage a nation.

Manipulation and deceit, with the backing of main stream media, and powerful wealthy donors, the democrats are using Gestapo-like tactics to quell any resistance, twist truths and news, and use the "mob" (or horde) of zombies to intimidate and harass opposition. Look at the antics they pulled during the 2016 and 2018 elections. Aren't they are doing the same in 2020? Yes, and worse.

Well, perhaps they are. Under the fanatical determination of Nancy Pelosi, the greater plan is to destroy the president and America, and she is pushing the democrat-led congress to get legislation enacted to alter the election. Under one of the provisions of the Cares Act (due to the Covid-19 China Virus outbreak), there is money to support the US postal system, but, the bill is altered to allow more mail-in ballots, something like 80 million mail-in ballots! A little unclear about the details as the bill is under heated debate, but it has shady undertones that could allow a great deal of fraud regarding the election. A mail in ballot has no verification at all. It is sent out to anyone and everyone, there are no signatures, no verifications, no way to assure it goes to a valid voter. It can be forged, or filled in by a boiler-room of workers to all vote for a particular candidate, and there is no way for the local voting authority to validate the ballot legitimacy. The mail ballot system and fraud go hand-in-hand, a perfect opportunity for abuse and dirty tricks. And it is already documented as happening in states that allow early voting. People that have been dead for years are receiving ballots, as are those that have since moved, and even pets! This is true and factual, look it up.

Now there are legitimate mail in ballots, called "absentee ballots". This mail in ballot requires the voter signature and verification, and there is a small amount of paperwork to fill out to "request" the ballot materials. This is a "verified" ballot. It has a less likely chance for foul play, although that can and probably does happen a little bit. The absentee ballot is important for our service men and women on duty overseas, or elderly people that have physical and health limitations that would limit them going to the polling location. There are other folks that can use this type of ballot as well, and that is fair and reasonable, and greatly appreciated by those that need that.

The reality is that mail fraud is real, do the research. Also check out the special investigation report by Glenn Beck on the Blaze TV channel (August 19, 2020). Perhaps exerts can be found on YouTube, but there is factual evidence to show the democrats are deep into manipulating this election. To sway people to vote for a candidate is one thing, but to commit fraud to change an election outcome, borders on revolution. This is serious. There are "current" stories of ballots being mailed to pets, parents that have long since passed away, and to people that have moved. What happens to these randomly sent ballots is anyone's guess, but the democrats have great and nefarious plans for them, just watch the stories that come about in the days ahead.

This is not the democratic party of JFK or even Bill Clinton. What was the welfare of the working man under the Kennedy-era Democrats, which was the cornerstone of the party, has given way to a radical socialistic dogma, with legions of brain-washed stooges (zombies) to carry out mob violence and sow endless discord. Rather than come up with solutions to fix an issue, or make lives better for the people, they use rhetoric and hate speech, and the double-standard, to advance a dark agenda. Is this what democrats want from their party and the party stewardship?

Voter fraud and identity thefts are on a national scale, according to many experts. This is one area where the democrats have opened up their bag of dirty tricks. During the numerous democrat voter registration drives, many of the registration cards will ask for birth date, address, and last four numbers of the social security number. That is sensitive personal information that is never anyone's business to know. Why is that needed?

As the Springfield, Missouri democratic office would reply, "that information is used for follow-up purposes". The scary prospect is that the personal information is being sold or used, to make fake voter registrations. And it does happen, and far too frequently according to various news stories. Personal information is an identity theft resource, that can (and has been documented) be used to fill voter registration boxes and vote tallies. If this is in fact true, and done in other places, then fake people can be set up as voters all across the country. And with little to no verification, fraud, in the worst possible way can occur.

Let's not forget the masses of "ballots" that suddenly appear after the vote tallies are completed, like in Palm Beach County, Florida, in Atlanta, Georgia, and in Arizona (just to cite a few). Were these real and honest votes, or "just in time" to sway the election results? That never happens to benefit republican candidates.

Remember the "hanging chads" in Florida? It was the 2004 presidential race between George Bush and Al Gore, where the Florida electoral vote might had gone to Gore if the "chads" were favorable. The particular ballot used a card punch system, whereby the vote cast was made using a pin or punch through the paper ballot. Sometimes the punches were only partially made, others had more than one punch (such s a change in vote), but this created a huge controversy. For months, ballot recounts and debates on how votes were cast, went on and on. Fake ballots and manipulated ballots appeared to further add confusion. The majority of these ballots were from the southern democrat controlled counties.

At least four of the nationally covered races from the 2018 mid-term elections, were highly contested by the democrats, resulting in one race over turned by suspicious means. Once the voting is over, within the time period allowed by law, that is the end, is it not? No, apparently not. But wait... "surprise, surprise, surprise", to quote Gomer Pyle from the famous TV show, when magically, thousands of untallied ballots miraculously appeared "after" the final vote count. And surprisingly, "All" of these mysterious ballots were marked for the democrat candidate. In all of these cases, the "misplaced" ballots were 100% for the democratic party candidate. How is that possible? That would be a statistical impossibility! Hmm, highly suspicious, and there was no way they were real. The only way democrats can win is to cheat? Shameful! JFK, where are you?

In four 2018 highly reported races, those for the governorships in Georgia and Florida, and for the senator seat in Texas and Arizona, the results were very close and won by the republican candidates. The democrats objected and contested them. This has happened now for several years, in almost every race where the republican candidate had won by a very small margin, the "miracle ballots" would magically appear. These new votes, have, or would have, pushed the other candidate over the top. This is fraud in the worst case.

In Arizona, signatures were not matching what was on record. Missing ballots suddenly appeared out of "manna", and the rightful republican winner of the race had then suddenly lost. A recount produced the ever-slightest victory for the democrat contender. This is no less a travesty to every ideal we hold as fair and impartial elections. This is yet another example of why voter ID laws can help stem the mischief.

In Broward County, Florida, Supervisor of Elections, Brenda Snipes, was again at the middle of the latest controversy. Suddenly after the election, when the democrat candidate lost the governors race, she (they) found thousands of missing ballots, all of which were marked for the democrat contender. The supervisor is to report results within 30 minutes after the polls close, and over 43 hours later, Broward and Palm Beach counties have not reported their legal results. And, to this very day, she is still running the elections affairs of Broward County, Florida. How is it that this democrat election official is not jailed for tampering with the election process? If it were a republican doing these things (for years now), they would be in jail. Where is the justice?

In fact, and reported on many news reports, a legal expert was brought in to contest the election result for governor. As the race was very close, the democrats again sought to change the outcome. It was reported this lawyer touted that, "the election result will be turned". And from there a legal fight and vote recount got underway. "They" claimed they found some hundreds of thousands of unsubmitted ballots just within the that single Florida county. No other county in the state has had so much controversy or "miracle ballots". This has happened several times over the past elections. If one were to do the math, that number of missing ballots, not only would have turned the governors race, but the added ballot count was far in excess of the number of voters registered on file in that county. This deceit is fraud of the worst kind, illegal in every sense of the laws we are suppose to be governed by. And yet, there was no investigation or prosecution of the wrongdoers. The rightful candidate for governor still won, but the democrats, under the leadership of Ms. Snipes in this case, tried every knavery to sway the election.

In earlier campaigns, 2000, she was accused of this same trick, controversy, of destroying ballots, missing ballots, and not removing ineligible voters from the records. And not to forget the 2004 presidential race, where the "hanging chads" volleyed the question of which the intentions of the vote were for. This debacle also centered in Broward County.

These are crimes against everything this country was founded upon, and crimes that were not investigated. It's all very fishy, and grossly dishonest. How is it that we allow these people to run elections, run our governing offices, and are given control over our lives?

Without fair and reasonable voter ID laws, elections can then be swayed, and illegitimate candidates will have subverted our right to vote in our otherwise fair and free election system. "Fair and free", that is the premise and foundation of the laws for this country. Different than for all other nations, even throughout history, the hope for elections that are not tampered with, to freely choose the candidates, and then privately make their vote, has been the greatest liberty America offers. Is that freedom slipping away?

Voter fraud in this key and critical election of 2020, could well be the powder keg that ignites the next American Civil War. Truly so, because tensions are high these crazy days in this country, with the China Virus (Covid-19), mobs of criminals burning and looting in the major (democrat-run) cities, and the inflammatory mainstream media fanning the divide between the people. The tinderbox hasn't been so close to exploding since 1860!

Voter fraud in this election can be that spark that ignites a very turbulent time for this country and for the otherwise peaceful change of power via the American election process. This is how it plays out:

NEWSBREAK: Election Coverage, Tuesday November 3, 2020. *"It's midnight now, and nearly all of the votes have been tallied. President Trump has secured the largest landslide in electoral votes in history, and a huge proportion of the popular vote. Joe Biden and Kamala Harris do not concede the race."*

The next morning, hundreds of lawyers hired by the democrat party file legal pleas contesting the "fixed" election. Thousands and millions of "late" ballots are received from the postal service, and the results tallied. The 99% of the ballots are for Biden and other democrat congressional races, and the lawyers are in a filing frenzy to dispute the election. The media is fanning the flames of conspiracy on the part of President Trump and the republicans. The republican lawyers file counter legal papers, and the fight is on. Uncertainty and controversy sparks mob violence (from the democrats), rioting and looting, innocent people are getting harmed, and crime skyrockets. The call for law and order is ignored by the democrat run cities, prompting marshal law and a federal response to restore order. Shots are fired, the crisis worsens, and the markets go into a tailspin as uncertainty and fear grip the nation. The violence and counter violence escalates through the end of the year. On December 20, when the Electoral College is to cast their votes from the November 3rd election result, Trump is declared the victor, yet the thousands of law suits prevents President Trump from continuing his duties. Nancy Pelosi, Speaker of the House, becomes the temporary president pro-tem, and enacts all sorts of crazy executive orders. The country dives into total chaos, normal life and business comes to a halt, the food supply is disrupted, and near anarchy grips the once proud and prosperous nation. America sinks into a total mess.

This is a very real possibility for the election of 2020. The details and such may not be quite correct, but the chaos and uncertainty will disrupt everything in life, and the country will be in an absolute mess. Will marshal law restore order? Will there be troops and bloodshed like this country has never seen before? Will the mail in ballot scheme achieve its purpose of destroying America, and giving way to a socialistic government?

The Freedom of Speech and Worship

The First Amendment, which outlines our freedoms of speech and spiritual worship, have gravely been restricted by "Hate Speech" laws, mob rule, and a horribly corrupt mainstream media. Say the wrong thing in a public place, and you can be sued and dragged through the mud by these so-called "social justice warriors". Some employees have lost their jobs by mere idle chatter. There are many cases where the freedom of speech is becoming censored.

During the recent riots where the terrorist gangs of Black Lives Matter and Antifa have been expressing more than peaceful protests, the media and politicians won't speak ill of their actions. But the actions of these groups show their true nature, and it's dark. Whether by fear or intimidation, or the threat of violence, the media and leaders rather turn a blind eye than address the truth. That is censorship. We don't live in China or Russia, and our leaders are suppose to defend our rights. The media used to be honest and impartial, but now are typically leftist propagandists.

Our Constitution guarantees every citizen the Right to speak out, and voice their thought. One can say nearly anything one wishes, without harming or lying about facts, or certain vulgarities. There are laws that limit defamation of character, protections of speech, and other legal concepts, governed by legal processes. It is the Right and liberty of a citizen to speak negatively, or in a cursed manner, towards the government or its leaders. One can do so, up until such speech incites violence, or interferes with someone else's free speech. That can become a fine line, and the courts are the process to balance such matters.

Periodically over a number of years, but very much these more recent years, speech is highly monitored and censored. There is an ever-growing cadre of terms and thoughts that seem to appear from the media and the myriad of vocal groups, which are considered "unfair", "racist", "hateful", and so on. Almost anything said by someone, especially from opposing leaders and politicians, are attacked by the media moguls and activists, to prevent "free speech". The leftists profess freedom of speech, until it counters their thoughts. It is a one-sided, "my way" form of non-discussion, often emotional dribble, that prohibits free speech.

Often the consequences of expressing an opposing view comes with threats of legal action, physical harm, censorship, fines, and even jail time. What? Yes, it is true, in many parts of our otherwise free and open society, if you speak out contrary to "their" thinking, you are "beaten up". Example: a child in school or college reads an assignment or a research paper professing the good qualities of some leader or event, that may be contrary of that teacher's liking. The student may be "lamb-blasted", to use an old term. There are many examples that children and students talk about, where the teacher punishes the student in various ways.

The same is true in many work settings, where open speech is shut down, and the employee can face firing or other actions. Many employers have "rules of conduct " or other limitations on speech or thought. If an civic leader or political candidate says something, they are blasted by the media or some group as being "racist" for instance. Everything is "racist this or racist that". No one can say anything about anything without "offending" or "hurting one's feelings". And to say anything means consequences of some type. Try speaking to an audience of students about the positives of the Southern culture. You might well get lynched.

Speech also refers to the written word. Write and post certain thoughts on Facebook or other social media platforms, and there can be grave repercussions. It is cited true also writing right-leaning or conservative, and even patriotic materials, where here on Amazon, thoughts can be banned or suppressed. It's crazy, in every arena, speech or written expression is more and more scrutinized. And done so often with consequence.

And who is doing this? Just watch the news, check out social media, it is these left wing activists and leaders. It is also much of the mainstream media, the "fake news" journalists, many business leaders, school teachers and professors, the Hollywood crowd, all of these people that defy discussion of a contrary opinion.

No Tolerance for Religious Thought

The same is true about ones spiritual worship. America is a land for anyone to worship freely as they so choose. Freedom of religion is essentially the second half of the First Amendment. But speak the name of Jesus Christ, and can you face persecution, punishment, fines, and possibly imprisonment. Prior to 1960, the Bible was freely taught in public schools, prayer was practiced, and nativity scenes marked the Christmas holiday season. After 1960, Bible teaching was ousted from public schools, prayer was later banished, and not long after that, the radicals took Christ out of Christmas. In 1980, the Supreme court voted to ban the Ten Commandments from being displayed in public buildings, like courthouses and schools. Is the freedom to worship, or at least the Christian faith, banned from the public view?

The radical cite Jefferson's thinking that government should be separate from religion, the "Separation of Church and State" thinking. But hear too, the radicals got it twisted around, a clear attempt to get God out of our lives. No, Jefferson was concerned that government should not instill a state-mandated religion, like the English crown did over the American colonials. Not the separation of church from State, but rather the interference of government in our religious choices. America is founded upon Christian-Judeo values, namely the Bible. Our laws and system of justice is all biblically based. Most of the Founding Father's were strong faith-filled Christian men, as were (and still many are) members at all levels of government. It is not that being of one faith is right or wrong, especially to be a believer working as a public servant, but being a person of faith in public service instills a sense of duty to serve the people.

But to incite any other religion into the public square, it brings praises of "tolerance" and "inclusiveness" by the social warriors. And then to shove down the throats of our children in public school, that Christmas is about everybody and everything (expect Christ), is a violation of the 1st Amendment. And God forbid our children from reading the Ten Commandments. They might actually obey them.

Gun Rights - Under Attack

The Second Amendment, which is referred to as the Guns Rights amendment, reads: "A well regulated Militia, being necessary to the security of a free State, the right of the people to keep and bear Arms, shall not be infringed". The point being, the people have the legal right to have guns (or other arms) for their self-defense, protection of their property (namely the home) , and family. Also, if the government gets too out of control, the people should be able to rise up and overthrow them (by force if needed). And, government is not to enact any laws that interfere or limit this right. What has happened?

Every few days there seems to be yet another tragedy involving guns. Whether right or wrong, the whole issue is highly emotional for some, which then obscures the facts or reality. The underlying issue is that those left wing activist groups shout for ever more gun control and total confiscation, versus our Right to keep and bear arms. It is powder keg that can very truly start another civil war.

Among the latest event, was yet another police brutality story resulting in the death of a black man. This time, it was a policeman in Minneapolis, Minnesota, not a shooting, but the incident resulted in the death of a young black man named George Floyd. The circumstances were tragic, but the result had been a wild flurry of angry mob riots and protests, not just in the city of Minneapolis where the incident took place, but nearly nationwide. And with that, the mobs went crazy, and the media and politicians cry out for more gun control, and with ever more animosity towards the police.

This particular event was horrible and tragic in every sense, and all us should bereave the loss of the victim. It is so tragic that in Our great country, these terrible actions occur, but they do. We have a free and open society, where wrongs will be made, but we have hope in our justice and electoral system will make things right and fair. For even a single moment, can we come together and lift up those effected in prayer? Can we strive to work together to bring healing and unity in the aftermath?

Apparently not. But more gun control? Will more laws solve the issue? In the aftermath of the George Floyd, the rift between those wanting law and order, versus those without any morale compass. It is more than a gun control issue, but guns are a part of the picture. We must have laws, and those people willing to defend and enforce the laws (like policemen with firearms). Otherwise, society breaks down into anarchy, where only the strong dictate the rules (and they do have guns). If these lawless bands can dictate to the politicians to defund (essentially disarm) the police that are suppose to protect us, then that defies many of our cherished rights, does it not? Where would fairness or justice be then? Mob rule, by force, and by what standards or edicts, "the law of the jungle"?

Without rehashing the details of the Floyd case, like the major media had done over and over for weeks, the matter is another sign that civil unrest is a powder keg in the gun control issue. Some refer to this case as police brutality, others cite racial prejudice and "white supremacy". Both sides may have merit, but if even of these criminals (and politicians) really cared about Mr. Floyd, police brutality, rights, or gun control, violence and riots is not the right way to push an a position.

The news media have shewed the truth of the incident, but basically what happened was a black man got into a confrontation with a police officer, and the officer used excessive force that killed the civilian. The particular force used was unwarranted according to the news media, lawyers, and the general public. The officer was subsequently charged with murder. This was despite the fact that the man was a former felon, with evidence of narcotics in his system, and that the struggle was something the officer had to do for his own protection. This was both a horrible and tragic situation, and no one ever wants this to happen.

But the result has been civil unrest and violence not seen for a few years, and has spurred on the controversy of the police, racism, and guns (in the hands of police). Violent protests and riots, destroying private property of individuals and businesses, along with physical violence against innocent people, then sprang up in many major cities for weeks. How much of this was for the wrongful death of Mr. Floyd? If these people really cared about Mr. Floyd, would they not be peaceful and melancholy?

Unnecessary police brutality in this case is one thing, but then this incident again brought up the whole controversy of police versus black people. The criminal groups of Black Lives Matter and Antifa, and perhaps others, were "allowed" to rampage through the streets of Minneapolis, looting and destroying property without consequence. The new demands by the riotous mobs were to "defund" the various police departments, which are suppose to protect lives and property from violence. Other cities also had protest marches, with rioting taking place in some of these.

Interesting to note, this prompted a case of illegal gun seizure occurred during the Floyd riots. As riots and protests were happening in many cities, in Saint Louis, Missouri, had an incident that should raise an unsettling :red flag". In Saint Louis, the peaceful protests quickly turned into a violent riot, with destruction of private property, businesses being looted, fires, and attacks on innocent people. The mob was then headed towards the mayor's home, on a private (not public) road, inside a private community, with iron gates.

The rioters broke down the gate, and were headed towards the mayors home, hurling objects (such as rocks), yelling and shouting, as they moved along. As they approached the McCluskey's home, the couple moved onto their porch with firearms. They called 911, but help from the police never came. Mr. McCluskey had a rifle (of some sort), and his wife had an (unloaded) pistol. Nothing happened as the rioters moved away, but several days later, the police showed up and confiscated their firearms, and the district attorney, Kim Gardner, charged the couple with some type of assault charge (a felony). Rather than stop the rioters or charge any of them for the crimes they blatantly committed, this democrat attorney went after the would-be victims.

Was that legal? Was it right or fair? There was the potential of violence, personal harm, theft, and destruction of their private home, by rioting criminals, yet the McCluskey's were charged a felony? Can you not defend your home, property, or even your person, from the potential of harm? And without having the police show up to defend you, you better have your own means

Now the McCluskey's as it was told, are civil right attorney's, which a strange irony to this civil rights like situation. What rights do they, or anyone have in such an event? At least in Missouri, there is the Castle Doctrine, the Stand Your Ground Law, and a law concerning brandishing a weapon. As the case gets national attention and eventually settled, the issue is one that greatly threatens everything the constitution is suppose to guarantee at its core. The rights to own property (home, car, and stuff), defend yourself (and family) from potential harm, and the ownership and use firearms to back up those rights, are exactly the whole point. We are suppose to have rights, unless politically motivated (too often democrat politicians) deem otherwise. This is real, research this yourself.

Essentially, if someone in public authority (like the district attorney in this case), can deny your inalienable rights, then do you really even have them at all? What does it take for any public or elected official to take your property (like your means of self defense) by some local ordinance, or broader law? What about if someone (like a neighbor or ex-spouse, co-worker, or whoever) says that "so and so" is a threatening person, and the police crash in and take away their guns? As simplistic and far fetched as that may sound, basically that is what the Red Flag laws allows the government to do.

The McCluskey case is different, in that it was local laws and the local attorney that initiated the seizure, but the idea of confiscation via the government, "under the law", is rather unsettling. The anti-gun advocates don't need to get rid of the Second Amendment, they just need to nullify it with laws and regulations. There are more and more cases where firearms are being confiscated via various laws, some rightfully so, but it denotes a frightening trend.

Shortly after the Floyd incident, another black man was shot and killed in Atlanta, Georgia by a policeman. Here too, there was a struggle between the police officer and the man, resulting in the officer shooting and killing him. This added more fuel to the current mayhem, and prompted an armed takeover of a portion of downtown Seattle, Washington for several weeks.

A mob of rioters took control of about six city blocks of downtown Seattle, Washington for several weeks. It was not a peaceful protest of the Floyd brutality issue, but was a violent mob takeover. They erected barriers to block entrance into the area, businesses and property were destroyed and looted, people shot and injured, plus other crimes. One known celebrity handed out guns. The (democrat) mayor and governor stood by and took no action to end the violence, and the media applauded the "festival" as a peaceful fun-loving event. That is exactly the point, that laws have no effect on criminals acquiring and using firearms for their own gain. And (democrat) politicians will do nothing to halt it.

And these violent riots were not limited to Minneapolis and Seattle, other cities saw similar lawlessness and total disregard for the law. If our governing officials will not protect the citizens, via the laws and rights enshrined, then they want more gun laws to do what? What can new laws do that criminals will abide by? If the government is there to protect the people from gun violence and crime, yet do nothing realistic to fix it, then they must be removed from office. To oust the government, we the people, must vote. Voting is our best method of fixing the problems in our society. America was founded on the principles of law and a due process, and the vote is the mechanism that peaceful change can come about. And the vote then empowers new leadership to enact laws and take actions that will protect the people and our rights.

During these crisis situations, the (democrat) city mayors, and state governors did nothing to intervene. Cowering to the mob rule, the democrat controlled government of Minneapolis have closed down the police department, by pulling their public funding. Instead of police protection, there is no protection for life or property, and the mob of criminals is free to do as they please? Is that right, just, or fair, no matter what color your skin is, or your background? Forget the rights of the people, the rights of property, or free speech, as the government which is put in power to protect our rights, won't uphold or enforce them.

And these violent riots were not limited to Minneapolis, Seattle saw similar lawlessness and total disregard for the rights of the people by democrat leaders. If our governing officials will not protect the citizens, via the laws and rights enshrined, then they need to be removed from office. To oust the government, we the people, must vote. Voting is our best method of fixing the problems in our society. America was founded on the principles of law and a due process, and the vote is the mechanism that peaceful change can come about. And the vote then empowers new leadership to enact laws and take actions that will protect the people and our rights. Make your voice heard, vote.

That is how our system of governing is suppose to work. Leaders are elected by the free-will of the people, to enforce the laws, for the good of society. Now in these situations where the mob has ruled that we the people should not have police departments, or property rights, or personal protection from violence, does that make any sense? Is closing police departments a service to the people, ending the inherent den of racism prevalent in law enforcement? The elected officials in these cities, like Minneapolis, Seattle, Washington DC, Baltimore, New York, Atlanta, and others, are acting upon the whims of the mob, versus serving the needs of those who elected them. In every case of violence and shootings of police and black men, over the past many years, has been in cities controlled by democrat leaders. Check the stats, check the numbers, this is true. Something about the fallen democrat party no longer serves the people or the working man like they used to. The Kennedy era democrats are done, and in their wake are terrible leaders that have let our cities crumble into ruin. Do the research, see for yourself.

Anarchy and mob rule violates our Rights of free speech, happiness, the ownership of property (including the shirt on your back), and the ability to pursue a peaceful and safe productive life. "The strong thrive, and the weak will submit to tyranny and oppression". That is not what America is about. Every man and woman must stand up and fight for our rights and freedoms, because the radicals are going to take them away.

Just a side note, is it that my thoughts and opinions are always derogatory towards the democrat party and those that align themselves as such? Yes, for the most part, but not exclusively. The republican party and many of those politicians and folks do at times exhibit disgraceful and shameful conduct as well. People are imperfect, and we all have flaws, and sometimes we do fall short. It's part of being a human creature. But looking at which side seems to cause more stirring and fussing, it's mostly the democrats.

Look at the acts, which cities have the largest problems, those that are democrat controlled. The highest crime, gun violence, etc., are democrat controlled. Who seeks more restrictive laws towards firearms, the democrats. Nearly every issue over restricting rights, freedoms, and liberties, raising taxes, expanding the size and intrusiveness of government, and control, they are democrat initiated. Do the research, check the records, this is true.

GUN CONTROL - AN EXPLOSIVE POWDER KEG

More gun control? With every shooting, police involvement or not, the anti-gun activists clamor for more controls, and getting rid of the second amendment. There are some 140 million gun owners in this country, and to threaten government seizure our weapons may be the spark to an all-out civil war, From law enforcement to ex-military, and the common man, having guns is vital for personal defense, and the protection of private property. The ideas of rights, and the unlawful seizures and further restrictions cuts right to the core of government taking away our rights, which should be resisted.

And with every publicized incidence, politicians come up with a myriad of crazy solutions, but continue to ignore the problem. There are plenty of gun laws on the books, good ones, but they are not fully enforced. Add a thousand more laws and regulations, yet it will do nothing more than keep good honest citizens from legally being able to protect themselves. also, more insane regulations and restrictions will further incite more illegal gun violence. On the other hand, criminals and illegal aliens are armed with all sorts of firearms, laws or not. A criminal will have all of the guns and bad stuff they want, laws or not. If criminals are able to have guns, but the regular honest person are not, then this too is a powder keg that could ignite the next civil war. It seems that the laws protect the criminals, but the honest folks are forced to prove their innocence.

Is it not so? Last year in Richmond, Virginia, there was to be a pro-gun, pro-family, pro-American rally. The rally was well promoted to the governor and the press about how regular people need to protect themselves and support for the laws. The governor, the media, and various anti-American groups all opposed the proposed rally, calling for police barricades and threatening bringing in the national guard, fearing that a gathering would be a hot-spot for "white supremacist" groups. Yet, this same (democrat) governor did nothing to stop the riots and violence that happened in Charlottesville.

If a conservative group, like those supporting pro-life, or pro-constitutional rights tries to have a march, then the (democrat) leaders, the media, and anti-American groups, opposes them. It is very clear, that when a riot happens, these same groups and leaders sing their praises and do nothing to support our rights or protect the people. Why is it upside down? And again, do the research yourself, and you will find, that it is the democrat leaders, mayors, city council members, and governors, that oppose the rights of people in favor of mob rule.

It is telling that the media and the politicians don't as much greave with the victims, as President Trump does, but instead they just cry out for more controls and gun confiscation. This was again the case with the George Floyd death in Minneapolis, and with the shooting death in Atlanta, shortly thereafter. The media, and these rioters care more about their anti-police, anti-gun bias, than they mourn for the victims. This facade by these leftwing people is very clear, which furthers the divide in this country.

These same clamorous groups demand intensive Universal Background Checks, limits on magazine size, eliminating certain types of weapons from the marketplace. These are the typical knee-jerk emotional reactions tat come about every time. There is increased talk about gun confiscation, often citing countries like Australia, and how it has "worked" there. Are these the answers? No! "Guns don't kill people, people kill people." Gun restricting laws do not save lives, but actually puts more people at risk. Restrict the good and regular law-abiding citizen from protecting themselves, and only the criminals and government will have guns. Does that make us safer?

In America, certain areas have high crime rates, other areas are less so, and the loss of life must never be down played. Life is precious, everyone's, not just one group or another, but everybody. All the laws in the world can never end gun violence. Why? Because criminals don't obey laws, it is that simple. Honest citizens follow the law, and adding more gun laws just hurts everyone. The bigger picture is simply this, the federal government does Not have the constitutional right to restrict or regulate our firearms. Yet, our rights as private citizens are greatly restricted by many federal laws. If the founding Fathers could only see how much we have shredded our county's establishment, they would call for another revolution. These are perilous times, and sadly, with every disastrous or tragic event, "We the People" eagerly surrender more and more of our freedoms to the mob rule, and to the central government.

The 2nd Amendment reads: "A well regulated Militia, being necessary to the security of a free State, the right of the people to keep and bear Arms, shall not be infringed".

What that means is that the feds are to "piss off" (according to one commentator), regarding any regulation of our firearms. Study the history and the intent of the founding Fathers when they wrote the Bill of Rights. They had a great document for establishing the new country, but they felt something more was needed to define individual Rights that the federal government should not touch. Everything else not specifically stated was to be relegated to the States.

The whole point of the revolution was that the central government was unjust and "tyrannical" in the abuse of governing powers towards the citizens. It was only because the citizens had arms, and took up arms, to defy the government, that there was a revolt. Without the governed having their firearms, the government would have simply used their armaments and force to squash any opposition. In fact, they tried, but the people fought back.

The government, the federal government at least, is not to limit or restrict this right. It is most closely related to the 1st Amendment of free speech, because the people have the right to speak out against the government, and to assemble (peacefully). Also the 2nd is closely associated with the 4th and 5th, as the people have the rights to own property and not be subject to search and seizure without due process. The more you read and learn about those early days of the nation, it was so important to spell out what the government did not have control over.

The point of this book is to alert and remind ourselves that we are a nation of laws, and that we as citizens have rights and freedoms guaranteed to us by our founding document, the Constitution. Rather than get into the "nuts and bolts" of the laws and proposed ideas of what and how new and old regulations work, my intent is to suggest that our "inalienable rights" are being squashed.

We, as a free people, need to educate ourselves, and determine for ourselves where and which way we want our governing leaders to guide us. It is through the power of your vote, which is your voice, to elect those leaders that uphold your values and traditions. There are a number of ideas and topics discussed that I hope to inspire you to learn more, and inspire you to do something (at least vote).

There is a humorous, but pointed story, that is greatly appropriate.

"A bunch of sheep were happily grazing in the field, enjoying the comforts of their lives. A wolf came out of the woods and killed one of the sheep. In a panic, they formed a consensus on what to do. They decided the best way to keep themselves safe was to remove all of their teeth. Later, the wolf came back and killed them all."

Get the picture? This is the push the leftists, the media, and the weak-kneed limp-wristed politicians are screaming for. Are we better off disarmed, or have some means to protect ourselves? Many say "No", and may ignite a civil war, should the right spark happen.

The Right to Fight - More about the Gun Issue

The modern day fight over Gun Rights is Not about having a few hunting rifles or shotguns. It is about the people being able to stand up against the federal government, with a counter-force, when said government becomes "tyrannical." Gun rights is also about the Rights of the people to have and own personal property (the 4th Amendment), the Rights of Free Speech and Worship, and assembly, and openly criticizing the government (1st Amendment), plus the others set forth in the original Bill of Rights. But it is the 2nd that really defends the others. It is made the second for a reason, it's important. Remember, our forefathers went through a long struggle with a governing body that prompted the whole revolt. They put together the best and most fair principles in establishing and running a country as ever has been written, with "the people" in mind.

According to a news story, America ranks about 53rd in the world for gun violence. However, to the "fake-news" media, America is the "only" country where guns kill people. Not true, not even close to being realistic at all. And every country has murder and assault crimes without guns, like stabbings, poisonings, and so on. To say that America is riddled with gun violence is totally misstated. It is no less a horrid part of our culture or human existence, but learn the facts. And factually put, guns stop a great many would-be crimes, but that is never talked about in the media. Do your own research and learn for yourselves what is true and accurate.

The larger cities have higher rates of violent crime, and those involving guns than rural areas with lower densities of people, obviously. Too often and in high proportions of the events, it is gang shootings, drugs and other crime related activities, illegal aliens involved in criminal actions, when most gun violence occurs. These criminals do not care about what laws are out there, what weapon bans are in place, as they will get the weaponry that they want. Again, do your research and learn for yourselves who and where gun violence occurs. Go talk with your local law enforcement, search for crime stats online. There is a lot of sources for information out there, so learn for yourselves. My intent is not to cite stats, but to incite discussion and questions for you to follow up on.

Many politicians and people are calling for more regulations, more intensive background checks, eliminating certain weapons from the marketplace, imposing more taxes on weapons and ammo, and other measures. Now President Trump is in a tough position, because he must do something. There are those who want him to do this or do that, but in the end, he will make up his own mind. Understand that Trump has been very supportive of our constitution and the rule of law.

Trump had appointed two originalist Supreme Court Justices, Gorsuch and Kavanaugh. Both have shown thus far, that they are strongly supportive of the constitution with a strict interpretation of the law, not wavering over the latest emotional frenzy. President Trump has also appointed almost three hundred federal judges whom also hold a conservative interpretation of the law. Should he be able to appoint yet another good Supreme Court justice, and more judges, then our rights will, or should be, better enforced.

Some politicians who cry out for more laws and restrictions, like Nancy Pelosi, Speaker of the House, are the ones who have controlled these crime-ridden cesspool inner cities for decades, yet have done nothing to fix them! If the laws they have imposed locally in their own districts have done nothing to stop or even reduce gun violence there, how well will their new proposed restrictions work on the country as a whole? This is a bad approach to fix the problems, they will not work. And real-life data will show how poorly the current laws are doing.

Fix the NCIC system. The National Crime Information Center (or NCIC) is a national FBI background check database, developed with guidance from the NRA (National Rifle Association), and is a good system. It is a system that works, if and only if, the law is enforced. Data will show that many states and local areas do Not fully input the data necessary. If it is not in the database, then the background check system does no one any good. Fix it. Make sure all of the necessary data is added, and that is the best solution to the entire background issue. If you go into a store to purchase a firearm, you will be subject to plenty of screening and background checks. If the system is handled as intended, those seeking firearms the legal way, should keep those purchasers on the "straight and narrow". Criminals don't care about the law. They will get all the weaponry they desire.

Mental health, that is the other key issue with gun-related violence. Among the leading causes of these people conducting the "mass shootings", is that they are mentally ill. Whether these men (primarily) are just under minor distress or frustration, or total "whack jobs", is irrelevant, they are sick and need help. How to assess a would-be shooter, the signs of mental illness, and then restrict them from obtaining firearms is the heart of the matter. That is very complex. In our free and open society, anything to infringe upon the liberty of personal choice borders on unconstitutional restriction of freedoms. But, laws are suppose to get enacted to protect us. Not to do something, "for the common good of the people", is not an easy option either, There has to be a balance in there somewhere.

Ok, for mental illness laws to work, one needs to define "what" constitutes a mental illness, and, is that grounds for the government to seize your guns? Many states, like California, used to have a strong mental health system. There was a system in place to help people with a wide range of issues, some of which might be valid grounds to keep firearms out of certain patients hands. Under democrat leadership for the last fifteen or twenty years, the mental health system was dismantled. Instead, many mentally ill people are turned out into the streets, and too many seem to get little or no care at all. This is true according to various law enforcement professionals, that statistics on homeless and the level of crime, do correlate. And as California goes, so goes the nation. Many other states have all but scraped their former mental health care, and the homeless problem and crime has increased. Some of these ill folks have used firearms in various crimes, including a few mass shootings, yet are still on the streets. How well will new guns laws work on mentally ill and homeless people?

Now, the mass shootings are the most publicized and politicized events, but the epidemic of gun-related crime in the country is often between individuals or small groups. Gangs, drug-related crimes, domestic violence, and so on, makes up the bulk of gun violent activities. It is no less horrible or tragic, and is also greatly difficult in resolving. Here though, there are laws already established, but need to be enforced. When a person or persons commits a crime (of any type), there are laws that are to be enforced. If the person is found guilty under the due process of certain laws, they are constitutionally banned from possessing or owning firearms. Such cases are those people convicted of felonies, or have been legally pronounced mentally unfit. There are a number of laws and rules relating to such banishment. But the point is, that if the laws are enforced, a great volume of gun-related violence would be stopped. The reality is, the laws are too often not enforced. And the justice system is mired in politics and double-standards.

There are two major areas where the laws should be strengthened and enforced, and they are the NCIC's system and illegal immigration. Both will have a dramatic effect in reducing the gun problem without infringement on our rights.

As mentioned, the NCIC system is a national database that is suppose to be updated (by human input) of those convicted of major crimes, namely felonies. That is a national system, controlled by the FBI, that is suppose to be available to every law enforcement location. Those people seeking a firearm purchase already have to pass a background check, which taps into the NCIC's system. If those people are there, then they are denied the gun purchase. No gun, then less likely a gun-related crime (at least for the law-abiding citizens). The problem is the data is not being input as it should. So a known criminal might be able to get a firearm.

Also a concern is how the justice system turns known violent felons back onto the street too early. Whether via loopholes in the system or politics, some of the most dangerous criminals are allowed their freedom. A large portion of violent and gun related crimes are committed by these known people, and they do not care about gun laws.

Regular and repeat criminals don't usually get their weapons from responsible means, so the NCIC's is less effective in that regard. Still, the system would be helpful in stopping a large portion of known offenders (in the NCIC system) and some mentally ill people from "legally" obtaining guns. The bottom line is that there is no way to stop 100% of gun violence in America, that can not happen.

If America is suppose to be a nation of laws, then that pertains to having a border that limits or prevents unwanted people from entering this country without due process. Our Constitution is very clear about a strong border, with the executive branch, the president, holding certain powers to enforce and protect it. The role of the president is to protect the citizens, and that is exactly what needs to happen at our own borders. No country in the world has an open border and such an influx of people, with no clue who or what these migrants may be. The reality is, that our southern border with Mexico is a mess.

Sadly, half of congress, mostly the democrats, have taken a hostile anti-Trump stance with anything and everything President Trump tries to do. Nancy Pelosi, Speaker of the House, is the worst and most disgraceful anti-American bigot in power. There are many other politicians, including many republicans, that are not serving the people as they should, and have done nothing but exasperated the divide between our peoples. The role of elected leaders is to represent the will and needs of the people, yet all many of these so-called leaders have whined and cried about their own political agendas, in their grab for personal wealth and prominence. And with that, our the powder keg rumbles.

Just like the little story of the sheep and wolf, the politicians would take away our teeth so we will "feel safe". Elections have consequences. You have to vote. You have to encourage others to vote, and get these dangerous and moronic politicians out of office. Make no mistake, the democrats and some of the weakling republicans are coming for your guns. Constitutional rights or not, we are just an election away from being disarmed.

Learn History

Now on the contrary, good decent law-abiding gun-carrying citizens have stopped thousands of (potential) crimes, exactly because they were armed. Rarely does the news media relay such stories, it doesn't fit their narrative. In America, it is Our legal and God-given Right to protect our property and ourselves. Our Founding Fathers knew exactly what was needed to be stated and sanctioned in the Constitution. An armed citizenry is a safer nation. Guns in the hands of responsible trained average citizens, has done more to protect life and property than all of the legions of police.

As our public school system has made great efforts to minimize and change the teaching of our history, our children are not being taught the full story. Our educational system today has all but eliminated the truths and realities of what actually happened in our past, under the guise of political correctness. History happened, and you can not change it, but if you don't teach it (correctly and honestly), history tends to repeat itself. The horrific events that led up to the rise of the Third Reich and World War II can again play out in America. Learn abut Cambodia, and the Chinese Communist takeover. There is a lot of recent history to learn about.

The path of every socialist, fascist, or communist takeover is very simple. First, make the children ignorant. Teach them about unicorns, sexual preferences, and the evils of capitalistic Founding Fathers. Make them stupid, and they become sheep. Take over the media, and control the narrative. Through the school and college system, raise future leaders that hold to "progressive" ideologies. Get elected into every public service office and erode the system from within. Banish God and religion from the public sphere, and promote state-offered benefits. Screw up the economy through debt accumulation and fighting needless foreign wars. Build the society around government handouts and dependency. Ban guns, and limit speech, and keep the people divided. Then in the midst of chaos, there arises a man with all of the answers and solutions. The people then take that bait, hook, line, and "stinker". The few in power then dictate every aspect of life, so as there is nothing left of individual freedom, thought, or liberty. The only recourse is revolution. How close are we in this country?

Go back and study history. Go on ebay or Amazon and find yourself a history schoolbook written in the 1980s or earlier. Read what was taught, and compare that with a modern school text. Compare and contrast, and if you could find a history book older than that, how does that differ? Older history books tell of heroic men, with an innovative spirit and hard work, tackling huge challenges, building this country in every aspect of life. Washington, Jefferson, and the other Founding Fathers were heroes, now called racists and other inflammatory falsehoods. These men formed America, and put together what they believed a country of free people should do, and know, to make their young nation strong and prosperous. They had spent years fighting the tyranny of government control, and specifically included a provision for the people to bear arms for their own defense. They knew, that without one's own ability to defend themselves, the government, or another person, would try to control or harm them. Even with other rights and laws in place, power and force has always been the bottom line in protecting personal liberty.

It is therefore so important we, and our children, learn history, true history, the good, bad, and the ugly parts of it. History happened, it's real, but more and more the facts and details are so watered down, the lesson is washed away. If you don't know what happened, how it developed into the myriad of events and outcomes, then you can not learn from the past. If you don't know the past, these events and lessons tend to be repeated.

Does anyone remember Nazi Germany and the Holocaust? Or was that erased from the history books also? Under the guise of law, the socialist controlled government (the National Socialist Party, the Nazi's) made it legal to round up groups of people they disliked, and under "the law", it was legal to kill them. The government sanctioned the murder of their own citizens. Of course, it wasn't called murder; they must have had some legal rationale, which made it acceptable. How many millions of German citizens did their own government murder, by law? Was it 3 million, 6 million? And it was not all people of Jewish heritage; there were

Christians and Communists, scholars and professors, and any political opponent the party felt was a threat.

How was that possible? The government took away the guns from private citizens. Confiscation by law, implemented by force, and the people were defenseless to stop it. Is that possible for the United States of America with it's Second Amendment to the Constitution, guaranteeing the Right of the people to own and bear arms? Of yes! It is happening here, and every day, and with every popularized tragedy, full of biased misinformation by the media, groups and politicians are clamoring for more gun control laws. Many of these folks are calling for the confiscation of guns by any means.

The Right for a private citizen to own and carry a firearm(s) is greatly threatened, and it is not necessary for the Second Amendment to be ousted off the Constitution. And that includes the stealing of your private property by the government if they confiscate your firearms. Add more laws, more restrictions, more conditions, limited the sale and production of weapons and ammo, just squeeze at the margins.

Long gone are the days when many of the high school kids (boys mostly) had rifle racks and rifles in their pickups. At least at the school I went to. More and more places disallow guns to be carried onto the premise, like government buildings, schools, movie theatres, more retail stores, etc. A "Gun Free Zone" designation by liberal democrat leaders will make us safer? Almost every single mass shooting occurs in gun-free zones. Gun-free zone tells a criminal, "come shoot here, no one will stop you". What about law enforcement? "There is never a cop around when you need one", an old cliche, but too often true. If one were to research and learn the true real-life facts about guns, gun safety, and crime, gun-free zones are death traps, and where citizens are allowed to carry guns, crime is greatly reduced. Guns, in the hands of responsible citizens prevent gun violence, which is factual. Learn for yourself, talk to your local sheriff or police officers, and research the public data.

THE BIGGER PICTURE

And actually, at stake is far more nefarious than just another racial shooting or gun law. With every chaotic event, we go through the same drama, which results in further losing our rights. The bigger picture is the assault on the Rights to Bear Arms, and the Rights of Personal Property Ownership. Certainly, Rights of Free Speech, to Worship freely, the Rights to Assemble, and others are also being stripped away. With each election, each tragedy hyped by the biased "Yellow Journalists", politicians, and the various "hate" groups, they gesture for more restrictive laws and regulations. This is true and has been happening more often.

This next election cycle will focus on more controls. It is interesting how the democrats want more controls, new laws and regulations, more taxes to fund ever larger government programs. Yet with years and decades of control of the large cities, crime and gun violence continues to increase. Where is the outcry from the media over inner city gang violence? There is a double-standard that these politicians and media apply to every issue, and it's always the republicans and conservatives at fault. Again, do your own research to see for yourself.

The bigger picture is this, there is a group of powerful people, working behind the scenes of every one of these side-show events, like the mob violence. Their goal is to destroy, or at least transform America into something very different, a totalitarian state, whereby a few elites control every facet of life. The plan was disrupted by Trump winning in 2016, and that has fuelled the campaign of Trump-hatred. Had Hillary Clinton won, as everyone was expecting, America would have been all but destroyed. The democrats would have been able to add two or three Supreme Court justices, that would rule by politics rather than by constitutional law, making it possible to change or destroy every freedom and right otherwise guaranteed. We could have been further engulfed into the wars in the Middle East, while Issus was growing unchecked. They were pushing for conflict with Russia and North Korea, while our military was grossly depleted. The southern border would have been further opened to any and all invaders, supported generously by our tax dollars. Taxation would have skyrocketed to pay for ever more "government give-aways", during the ruined economy Obama created. With the nation in total chaos and disaster, controlled by a politically motivated court, the change into a socialistic society could have happened.

Far fetched? No, this is very real, very scary, and the democrats are even openly clamoring about the radical changes they want to do. The only things holding them back is President Donald Trump, and the freedom-loving patriots.

Now with all of these chaotic events and crises happening, we have the 2020 election. If President Trump is reelected, half of the country will cry "foul". The democrats have thousands of lawyers ready to file their dissent to the outcome. Now if Biden wins, half of the country will cry "voter fraud". So waht will happen? Watch. This may well be the spark that touches of the Second American Civil War.

What Can you Do?

How do we, as common individuals, make a difference? Vote. Our best and easiest way to do something of value is to use your voice via our Right to vote. Hopefully, there are candidates worthy to vote for, but the point is this, the vote is how change can and does come about in this country. We are a nation of laws, and we have the Constitution that outlines exactly how to make the nation function and the periodic changes in leadership is via the vote.

"Use it or lose it", because the democrats have demonstrated over and over again that they want more government, more control over every aspect of daily life, everyone dependent on a government handout or program, with fewer and fewer individual liberties. This again is factual, just look at the latest group of candidates running for office. What do they say, what do they stand for, and what have they done in the past? Do they adhere and support the constitution, or promote bigger government?

By not voting, be complacent, because you may be displeased with the choices of candidates, is the same as voting or the other side. If you don't vote, the opposing candidates are winning elections, and many of them want to destroy every constitutional right we have. This is fact, look, read, research, and learn for yourselves what is happening.

And who are being elected. Those gaining political and legal power (to make laws that govern our lives) has been going to liberals, progressives, socialists, and dishonest deceptive politicians. They seek power and riches, and in absolute contradiction to our established liberties and freedoms. Many of these folks are democrats, although to be fair, not all democrats adhere to the new radical party platform. Many republicans and other politicians may be vile snakes as well. There are poor leaders that call themselves republicans and independents also. Please don't misunderstand that! Overall, the New Democrat Party is a very different party than what existed before. And because these people are gaining office, they are making laws, some of which are very bad laws.

Liars, and Hypocrites

Some of these ideas and thoughts are repeated over and over. That is done purposefully, because they are important to hear. My hope is that you glean some thought provoking questions, and that you will seek to learn more, and do more. At least vote, and encourage your friends, family, and everyone else to vote as well.

The tragedy of America, in all its splendor and glorious "free and open" society, is that a few "bad apples" take advantage of the "goodness" that America was founded upon. This country was founded on the cornerstone of Christian-Judeo principles of doing good and right to others, to allow them the freedom of personal choice and the opportunity to rise above, to make their lives better. This is done without the heavy hand of rulers dictating every aspect of life, or with cruel oppression.

In this country, public officials take an oath of office to abide by, and uphold the statutes of the constitution, as their very basic requirement. It is a promise to work for the good will of the people that freely elected them. Yet in such openness, it is too easy for power, greed, and corruption to turn everything good and right about America, into the tyranny it is suppose to suppress.

What are today's biggest social issues? The democrats (and some republicans) say it is "white privilege", racism, police brutality, gun violence, global warming, and the outdated constitution. These leaders cry out for tolerance, fairness, better schools, and so on, but what is the reality? Look at every major city or problem area, and see who is in charge. The majority of these areas are controlled by democrats, many whom have been in power for decades. These leaders have had money, power, and the office to make changes for the all of the electorate, but nothing seems to get done. Why is that? For decades, these politicians make campaign promises, blame the republicans or the "racist system", but upon reelection, still nothing changes. The cities get worse, falling further into decay and depravity, otherwise ignored by the civic leaders. How is it that these clowns are able to stay in office?

In real life, look at people like Nancy Pelosi, who controls San Francisco. I was there years ago, used to ride the trolley cars, eat on the wharf, and drive all through the city. It was almost like a magical theme park. For the past decades of her control, the city has become a disgusting sewer of drugs, hoards of homeless people, crime, and human waste everywhere. Yet Nancy sits safe and sound in her high walled tower and armed guards, and has become wealthy at the citizens expense. She and her cronies, bilk ever increasing taxes from businesses and the common worker, controls the media, and screams for more gun laws and regulations. Did she ever take the oath of office? For many public "servants", it's hard to see based on their actions.

It is the same with the city of Baltimore under Cummings, Chicago under Ron Emmanuel, Bill deBlasio controlling New York, and so and on and so on. These places are a mess! The (democrat) rulers have become rich kings, catering to the wealthy desirable areas under their rule, yet neglect the poor neighborhoods, which are war zones. Here also, they clamor for more taxes and regulations, control of crime and gun violence, yet they use the propaganda of the media to retain power. Every city, every "hotspot" of crime and problem, these elected hypocrites have used power and the taxpayers purse to fatten themselves, to the suffering of the people. Shame on them!

These wealthy elitist politicians control the media, with support of wealthy patrons, so decades of control benefit the few, at the expense of the masses. And who are the ones most abused and neglected? Often it is the African-American and Hispanics, for whom these leaders claim to support. Tragically, they are no more than slaveholders, like the democrat leadership of old.

Shame on these politicians. They took an oath of office to the electorate, stewards of the public trust, yet they have abused their positions, and regulate away our liberties.

The hypocrisy of the media, and the so-called Hollywood elites is also widespread. Here these rich and famous movie moguls, and unknown actors and actresses, put on splendid award ceremonies and fund raisers, bashing the president and everything good and noble, in the name of ending racism and "social justice". These actors, mostly the women, spew hatred towards anyone opposed to their idealized utopian thinking, yet are the greatest of hypocrites.

During the riots in Minnesota and Washington, the jet-set crowd again made big speeches, spewed vulgarities and garbage from their lips, calling for radical changes in society. If these hate-mongers truly believed in these endless causes to right the wrongs of society, like police brutality in the inner cities, then prove it. Do they donate their own wealth to help anyone? If they cared, they would put their millions where their big mouths are. Has any of these leftist social warriors given all of the wealth to help their causes? How about 50%? !0%? Now money given to the lawyers to do the legal harassments, or money to put on yet another gala or award program, does not count. If they believed in helping the poor, the oppressed, then where is their money, their labor, and why are they never seen in the trenches getting dirty? Maybe because they are acting. The Hollywood elites are pretend, they are actors, playing a role of social warriors, until the day is done, and they go back to their wealth and luxury.

It is always the case, that leftist social changers, politicians, and all of these various groups want change, and demand money to "fix" the problems, but never contribute themselves. They always demand that someone else, like the taxpayers (who earn their own way), or the "rich" pay more to correct the disparities of society. Never themselves.

Bernie Saunders during his ill-fated attempt at running for president (a second time), shouted and pounded his fist demanding that more money get spent on some social injustice. When asked how much money he has contributed, he belatedly said "none". He is worth millions, so if he believed in such a great cause, then where is his support? Do insist that "we" pay for something without putting up your own resources first.

The battles in this time of unrest is between the "haves" and the "have nots". The "have not" side, wants what the "have" own, to make it fair and equitable. The redistribution of wealth is not a fair solution, but rather a socialist dogma.

The Black Lives (Don't) Matter Movement

The powder keg of racism, promoted by democrat politicians (and some republicans to be fair), the media, the Hollywood elites, and hate groups like Black Lives Matter (BLM) and Antifa, are close to bringing about a race war, if not a full civil war.

Yes, black lives do matter, of course they do! But so does white lives, red lives, brown lives, yellow lives, and every other color one might be. Blue lives matter, absolutely! Listen, all lives matter, but to say that only one group matters, and everyone else should bow down to them, that's "racist"! Read the doctrine from the BLM website, and read the disdain they have for all life, even black lives! The hold to plan of destruction of everything good and decent in this country, so beware. By marching around, causing the violence they do, they are showing who they really are, terrorists and thugs.

The group Black Lives Matter has promoted their slogan for several years now. Although it sounds good, the truth is that their organizational philosophy is anything but forthright. On their website, they oppose other black people if they disagree with their mantra. They disavow black policemen, they shun black republicans, and of course black conservatives. They favor the abortion (murder) of black babies at any time during the pregnancy. They are for dissolving the modern family. For a group that preaches that black people's lives matter, in fact, is misleading. If they cared, they would embrace "all" the people of color.

These groups and individuals can make a positive difference for race relations, and for improving the lives of people, but instead they clamor hate speech to the cheers of wanna-be socialist college students, and with support from the media. Protest rallies and riots where speakers spew vulgar hatred towards the president, "whites", cops, and anyone who opposes them, does not inspire change. Such actions only further the divide, making effective change less likely. Their only recourse is to become more violent, drawing more media attention. Certainly, change can be made, but not via the radical agenda.

Does anyone remember Ghandi? He spent half his life preaching peaceful change (the Indian liberation from British rule), and he abhorred violence. Through peace and love, he started a movement that brought about the greatest of changes, with hardly any violence. We can learn a lot from his teachings, and perhaps the great social divide can be breached.

Socialist versus Patriots - The Grand Strategy

Could the ideological divide of socialism versus constitutional rights be a powder keg to set off the next civil war? It is said by some, that there is a Grand Strategy, not just to take away our rights to bear arms, but all of our rights and freedoms.

As you listen to the media, the leftist leaning politicians, movie stars, and wacko's of every other sort, they are seeking a new utopia, with equality and fairness, and everything for free. There is a more publicly vocal group, the activists, seeking radical ideas, which is contrary to everything America is based upon. The goal is mass redistribution of wealth, a mass "Robin Hood" theft of property and rights, to make everything "fair and equitable" for all, even those who didn't earn it. There is a push to "end racism" by destroying statues and monuments, and erasing history. There is a movement for anarchy, since law enforcement is controlled by the "evil white man". To divide and vilify one group after another, to fight against traditions and everything stable and normal, are all socialist tricks.

The grand plan is destroy America. We nearly saw it come about under the Obama/Biden leadership 2008 to 2016, where strife and division was the excuse for more controls and regulations. It was a real life push to turn America in a socialist country, controlled by a few powerful players. And as all socialist countries go, the turn to communism (totalitarianism) soon follows. In the process, rights, freedoms, and liberties become fewer and more restricted, and then eventually made null and void. Private gun ownership and the Second Amendment are really the lynch-pin that stands in the way.

Remember the Revolutionary War? Not much of it, it's roots, or only a few of the details are taught in school anymore. Now it is viewed as "racist" or "unfair", so keeping with the doctrine of "dumbing our children down", such topics are merely a mention. Our forefathers fought for the freedom from tyranny (the English King at that time) that controlled every part of daily life. It was the rebellion, regular citizens armed "with guns" that made it possible. Now as the politicians are tightening the noose on our rights of self-defense and freedom from a tyrannical central government, so history is poised to repeat itself again. That can only lead to total surrender, or war.

Most striking during the Obama/Biden years was how he (and others, like the media) divided the people. We were staunchly united after 9-11, but he used race and income to divide us into smaller groups, pitting one against the other. It was black against white, brown against white, poor versus the rich, the evil big corporations against the poor, and so on. Divide and conquer, is a trick that works every time.

The strategy is very clear, first divide the unity of the people. Use the media to misinform, and as propaganda, to spread distrust and discord. Change the educational system to make the next generation "dumb", dependent on government, and stifle individualism. Teach evolution, sexual preferences, tolerance for everything except God, and the fantasy of a "unicorn utopia". Teach everything except the characteristics of our forefathers, hard work, independence, perseverance, and faith. Our children are confused, no idealism, no incentive to be innovative, become leaders, or to build. Want to take over a country? Start with brainwashing the children. Zombies make good "brown shirts".

Then take God out of the picture. America and western civilization is founded on Biblical truth. But get rid of the dependence on God, our moral compass, and the people will be lost and scattered like sheep. They will look to themselves, distractions of every type, and moral relativism to discern right from wrong. "Everything is acceptable, with no consequences or condemnation, just be tolerant". Sound familiar?

Next, take away the guns. Without a counter force, the private ownership and Right to defend yourself, then the tyranny of government will take control. History has shown us over and over, that this is true. Those without guns, will be subject to those that will use them.

With the people divided, our prodigy dumb and aimless, disarmed, then all you need is a "crisis". With a crisis, such as "climate change", the people will turn to a strong leader with all of the answers to fix everything, and solve all of the ills of society. And with that America is destroyed. Again, does anybody remember the rise of Nazi Germany, and their savior, Adolph Hitler? How about the communist takeover of Russia, Mao and China? Who was Paul Pott, and what did he do? Erase history, and you will repeat it.

Our guns are the tools to protect all of the rights and freedoms we are guaranteed by our founding document. We, as the people, need to act. We need to learn for ourselves what is happening, relearn history, contact our leaders and politicians and help them understand our concerns. We need to vote, and encourage others to vote as well. We need to arm ourselves, train, and perhaps join like-minded organizations. And certainly, we all need to get our knees and pray for wisdom and guidance from Almighty God.

What about Abortion? A Powder Keg?

If there are forces, people, politicians, and groups, that are trying to change America, wanting to take away individual rights and freedoms, could that trigger the next civil war? Allowing mob rule to take away the rights to defend ourselves may be that spark to blow the keg. But what about when it comes to family, and the rights of life?

The media and the leftist elites that push for gun control, are the same ones that enact laws to kill babies. On the one hand they call for help for illegal alien children at the border, but turn around and enact laws to kill our own citizens.

Again, they play the double-standard, and profess needing equality and fairness for all. Yes, there is an epidemic of gun-related deaths, but what about abortion? If a criminal with a gun attacks you, and you do not have one, then you become an innocent victim. What about a baby, the most precious and innocent of all life, murdered in cold blood, under the guise of legality? Which is worse, or what's the difference? In America, you have the Constitutional Right to defend yourself, even with a gun. But who defends a baby?

The recent New York State abortion law, essentially sanctions death to their citizens. Human babies can be killed late in the pregnancy, and even after the baby is born and takes its first breaths. This became law also in Virginia, with the approval of the democrat governor that has demonstrated how he supports chaos versus law and order. This same governor has been caught on video in bad behavior, but media and his party chooses to turn a "blind eye". There is something very wrong when our elected leaders usurp the common morality and traditions of the nation, and dishonor the oath of office they have taken.

Up until now, every statute in this country would call these late-term abortions as murder! Not anymore. This is a violation of our Rights of Worship, Speech, and the pursuit of happiness, and other guarantees as laid out in the constitution. Other states like Vermont and California has wanted similar laws. The deceptive politicians and some within the legal establishment will profess the contrary, but they are vicious liars and murderers.

We are a nation of laws, and the rule of law is the intent of how our leaders are suppose to govern our society. But laws are made that are not always good or right for the people. All abortion laws are legal, but none of them are right. It is by the twisting and perversion of right and wrong by filthy lawyers and crooked politicians that has brought us to this point. It is time to act and do something.

The majority of these politicians are democrats, but includes weak limp-wristed republicans also. Look at the voting records, it is very telling. These are the same hypocrites that cry out about the injustices of handling illegal alien children being held by border control officers, or those crying to "save the planet". But when it comes to killing human babies, our own citizens, these people and the media remain silent. They have traded their morale compass for humanistic ideals?

Do you think these elected officials care about your gun rights, your freedom to worship, or to speak against evil? Do you think they are upholding the statutes of the constitution? Whatever the issue, gun laws, rights of life, illegals crossing into our country, what is happening is the shredding of the foundational principles and protections laid out in the constitution. The more they create new laws, the closer America will become like Nazi Germany.

And what about a child's "the right to life"? The abortion question, is not just a freedom of religious worship, but it is also a freedom of speech. Perhaps the greater overall question is whether it is right and lawful for the government to kill, or sanction the killing, of its own citizens. Although the Supreme Court allowed the ability to kill unborn babies as a rule of law in Roe vs. Wade, is it right? No, it is a disgusting and abhorrence to everything good and honorable that this country touts to be. Murder is murder.

An unborn child is still a human being, up until now. How can these wise lawyers in the Supreme Court, who are charged in upholding the constitution, allow such debauchery? Because liberal presidents appointed liberal-thinking justices into the court, so poor laws get enacted and enforced. They care nothing about the Rule of Constitutional Law, but instead focus on the emotional political fad of the day. America is heading down the road to destruction if this trend continues.

When the States of New York and Virginia passed the new laws allowing the death of babies, the voting assembly members applauded the new laws with resounding glee! It is said that liberty will die with resounding applause. Soon, more states will enact laws contrary to tradition and justice. That is sounding more like Nazi Germany, the Soviet Union, or China. Are we really there?

Whether life begins at conception or when a baby draws its first breath is irrelevant. The question is how can we as a nation allow the murder of our own innocent and defenseless citizens? We are suppose to be a nation ruled by law, but not all laws are good or just. Where is the sanity of our lawmakers? This is murder, plain and simple. We need to act.

Elections have consequences. You vote for good people to lead us, that defend life and liberty, or not. We have seen the definitions of right or wrong changed to suit the desires of the mob, and by elected officials. You vote for your hearts desire, and apparently it's for death. And to have such leaders in power, they will continue to enact laws that will subvert and limit more of our rights.

Now if this horrid lust of killing innocent life is not overruled, then the rights of free speech, religious worship, and "the pursuit of happiness", are made mute. Our freedoms as guaranteed under the US Constitution will be destroyed. Those lawmakers, supporters of such legislation, and any group or organizations that adheres with such, are murders and co-conspirators. Then if this persists, then truth and justice in America is a lie!

What follows next? Well, because the murder of babies is made legal, the next step is to broaden that "definition" of whom can be (legally) murdered. Next will be young children no longer wanted by their parents, or perhaps the elderly will be killed at the whim of a politician. Then from there, any opposition group or segment of citizens, like white males, Christians, deplorable Trump supporters, and so on, can face the death squads (by law). "When the sword is unsheathed, it is difficult to put it back without first spilling blood."

Here also, if and when the government is allowed to restrict your rights to own firearms, or takes them away completely, then there will be no more questions about religion, free speech, abortion, rights to assemble, protests against the government, and so on. The Second Amendment is the Second one for a reason, it's important. The right of the citizens to defend themselves against a government that goes crazy is vitally important. It is the private ownership of firearms by the common people that protects the freedoms and liberties guaranteed in the Constitution. Without our Right to Bear Arms, how can we defend against tyranny?

"Those who gain power will abuse it, and then they will oppress the people, which then they will start murdering the citizenry." Strongly ponder these thoughts, it happened throughout history.

MORE ABOUT LOSING OUR LIBERTIES

Is it possible to lose our Constitutional rights and freedoms? These are guaranteed under the law, aren't they? Yes, but no.

With each election, it results in more radical thinking politicians taking office, by which they get laws and regulations passed to restrict our gun ownership, for instance.

Similarly with the rights of worship, there are increasing limits on what can and can not be publicly done (or seen). Not so long ago, one could pray in school. The Ten Commandments were posted in every courtroom and on most public buildings. Christmas and the name of Jesus were commonplace during the Christmas Holiday season.

Now, by laws and restrictions, it takes lawyers and legal battles to be able to meet on a public campus to have a time of prayer. How about courthouses are being stripped of the Ten Commandments, for which our laws are based upon. There are groups that make all sorts of claims of abuses and unfairness, but they just want anything Christian removed. How about last Christmas? How many battles did these atheists groups and organizations fight to demand the end of Christ-mas?

There are news stories where anti-Christian groups would set up satanic emblems and decorations next to Nativity scenes. These are all attacks on our constitutional rights of free worship. Apparently to many of these groups, everything is tolerated except Christianity, or anything that invokes the name of Jesus. These are the same groups that preach tolerance and free speech (except Christ).

Our freedom of speech, part of that 1st Amendment Right, along with Religion, is also greatly under attack. What about the Freedom of religious worship? Our Judeo-Christian roots that bore this country and our entire legal system have been greatly under attack as well. We are free to worship whom and what we like, or nothing at all, without the interference of government mandating what we can do. The idea of "separation of Church and State", has been grossly misrepresented by those seeking to abolish Christianity in America.

Thomas Jefferson and Hamilton had written about this matter from the beginning, citing that "not separation from government", but rather that "government shall not impose a religion". In other words, government would not declare a State religion. Being a person of faith, whatever you believe, and part of the government structure, should not be an issue. It is, and watching every Supreme Court nomination hearing, and even most Cabinet level screenings, there are those people, mostly the democrats, that scream about the separation of Church and State. Having a person that holds a belief and moral compass in public office is a good thing. Look at the corrupt lying politician filth currently serving in office, and then decide which is better.

If democrat politicians (who have the mission to control the lives of the people) are elected, they will enact more laws to reduce or eliminate the rights and privileges we hold. And in particular our freedom to speak in opposition, our ability to freely worship, our rights to bear arms, and so on. As we lose our freedom of speech (again as an example), we become slaves to the government. And what happens if there is no accountability? Dictatorship. No freedoms, the government becomes all-powerful, no opposition, and they hold the sole power of life and death over every citizen. Study human history, it's scary.

Don't the republicans seek control also? Yes, sure they do, as all that are elected are subject to the lusts of power and control. It's just that in recent times, the democrat party has become so radical in their quest to control people by restrictive laws and regulations, they have become totally nuts. Is that right or even fair? Some think it's fine, others are less happy, but the movement towards a socialist and totalitarian slavery will end all of the liberties and freedoms we still have.

This trend in our elections and the types of people elected to office is actually very scary. Too many are pushing for a government led and controlled society. Recent polls of college students suggest that about half favor socialistic ideals. Do our kids even know what they are talking about? If history and civics are not taught truthfully, how can they answer such questions? All countries that have embraced that style of slavery are unproductive, with a people that are oppressed. Why do you think illegal immigration is at an all-time high? Those nations embracing governmental control, historically, have not remained very long.

OTHER FREEDOMS
TO LOSE

Our gun rights or freedom of speech are not the only rights we can lose, but all of the others as well.

The Right to bear arms is one part, but the Rights of Private Property ownership are greatly threatened too. The Second Amendment protects the citizens' right to bear arms, for personal and family protection, but also to stand against tyrannical rulers. This fight has escalated in recent years, flamed by the biased media, and outspoken elitists. Here too, the critics claim that having guns is unsafe, yet those individuals have armed security and walled homes. More common than ever before, is the talk about gun confiscation, "Red Flag" laws are, and will become common, where "the government" can barge into your home and seize your guns. Without the Rights of private property or due process, under these unconstitutional laws, you're toast! Without the Right to defend yourself, do you think the rights of speech or worship will remain? Once the people are disarmed, then the government will become vicious. Study history. Again, recall the rise of Nazi Germany, communist Russia, and bloody China.

Also, beware the "Red Hat" laws. They are unconstitutional, at least if implemented by the federal government. Many states are implementing what is called Red Hat laws, whereby any person can simply accuse another person of being "dangerous". This then triggers law enforcement to confiscate that accused persons' firearms. Based merely on hearsay, without proof, and without due process. Is that not a violation of many of our personal rights and freedoms? Yes, and it is yet another way the leftists are starting to "void" the Second Amendment, rights of private property, and due process. One then has to fight to prove their innocence, versus proving guilt. Are you no longer innocent until proven guilty? In too many cases, you are considered guilty until you can prove yourself innocent. That is contrary to our rights.

As you look at the history of every nation that has turned socialist, the final thing the government would do is to remove the guns. Remove the ability of the citizens to fight against injustice, and the people will be easily controlled. Remove the guns, and all other rights and freedoms can not be defended. Again, take Nazi Germany for example. There was strong active opposition to the rise of the socialists, but once the guns were seized, the Nazis eliminated all of the critics. And we are talking about the government killing its own citizens. It is that scary.

How about the Rights to Assemble, Freedom to speak out against the government, worship, due process, and more? Could meeting at church be met with armed police or death squads? Not yet in America, but many places around the world, yes! Christian persecution is literally a life or death struggle in many countries. That can happen here too! Elect leaders hostile to the Christian faith, and watch what happens. Previously, there was a law that the preacher could not talk about politics or governmental actions in the pulpit. That has been removed, thanks to President Trump, so the truth and politics can be talked about openly. But that can change back again as well.

The Party "Not" for the People, or Life

The new democrat party promotes an "open door" stance in regards to borders and immigration, government oversight of religious values, control of education, a government sponsored health care system, highly restrictive gun ownership (if not outright confiscation), and a crackdown on freedom of expression. They encourage government programs to take care of every need, including income equality. They elevate the status of illegal immigrants, including the criminals and child-slavery bondsmen, over legal and natural American citizens. Life of the unborn has no rights, and therefore can be slaughtered almost at a whim. The new party promises higher wages via the redistribution of wealth, taxing the evil rich (white) aristocracy. Is this what people want from their governing bodies?

The radical wing uses slogans and bold words to promote their beliefs. "Be tolerant of other people and their lifestyles." "Save the planet by ending fossil fuels." "The government is your family, your provider, and your god." The bottom line is, they want a government controlled socialist State. The decisions and policies for the people, made by an elite group of "honorable intelligent" leaders, as they know best how to govern the nation, and each citizen. They promise the "good life", without the worry of consequence. Research and learn for yourself, who and what the new democrat party really stands for, but they do not stand up for American or Christian values.

Wake up Brethren. Wake up America. This is happening. Over the past several decades or so, we have seen so many traditions and what we would call Christian values being eroded. Look at marriage for instance. In the 1940s and 50s, divorce was not very common. Now, at least half of all people have been divorced at least once! Socialistic teachings, human-centered, sensitivity (or tolerance) training, are forces seeking to sway voters into this "progressive thinking". Anything to take the focus off of Christianity, and put it on world values, have eroded every traditional norm. The erosion of everything American is very real, and about to sink this nation. Many pastors say, "we are one generation away from losing Christianity in this country". It's true, look at church attendance. Most are nearly empty, and the few that attend, are mostly older folks. Youth, there are some, but not many. Sports and entertainment venues are packed, but the churches are empty and closing. Total erosion of this country's' foundation is real.

The new democrat party aligns itself to bold speech with no substance. The party for the people is no more. The new party uses violent speech and divisive rhetoric to stir up the masses of brainwashed zombies to overthrow society, on every issue of tradition, law, and freedoms. The new party professes the goodness of socialistic ideals, no support for the rights of life, but whitewashes the realities of repeated historical failures. Condemnation without solution. The "Peoples Party" is no longer the party of the people, but by Elitists, pushing to overturn the rights of gun ownership, free speech, worship, the rule of law, and equality for all. They are indoctrinating of our school children with the ideas that "government provides", versus hard work, family tradition, and merit through achievement.

This radical departure of traditional norms relates exactly to every election, where more and more districts and States are turning blue. Turning blue, or democrat, was not a bad thing, but the Kennedy-era Democrat, the working man's party, is long gone. The general populace is being brainwashed by empty promises that touts restriction and control, unsubstantiated opinion over logic and reason. Yet the vote turns blue, more and more often. It's like in the movies, when the people change from normal into zombies, and the power of the individual is given over to mass hysteria.

If this country is to be changed, let it be changed, through the process of law as it was founded. But what is changed, may not be what is good or right, or fair. And what changes, is not easily changed back. If traditions are deemed wrong, and what we have previously known as failed ideologies become entrenched, then individual liberties are restricted. The new rule of law becomes contrary to those established by our forefathers, and that seems to embrace evil over what we used to call good. And as power becomes concentrated in the hands of a few, there is no freedom of worship, freedom of speech, or anything else. Power is given over from the people (the individual), to the elites in government.

Who, or what groups adhere to what you hold as good and right? What you believe in, and the rights and privileges you enjoy, are just a few votes away from being changed. Think for yourself, and decide in the way that works best for you. Align yourself with those that hold those principles and ideals you want. And of course, pray. Pray for wisdom.

Whether it is of hyped rhetoric, or emotional dribble and fear, many groups vote based on superficial perceptions. Facts and realities don't assure votes any longer.

Now what is so wrong and bad about the democrats? "That is a biased and 'racist' statement. Only dumb religious fanatics and red-neck Wal-Mart shoppers would say such things. Obviously they are degenerate deplorable Republicans. What difference does it make if a county or state is Blue or Red, democrat or re-publican, that's just politics. At the end of the day, people are just trying to get through the day, free to do their own thing. Who should care which political party is in office, it has nothing to do with daily life." What? Who should care? All of us. It comes down to personal choice versus government edict. Think about it.

That is the whole point, it makes all the difference! It makes a difference who leads us. The values and principles our leaders have, and how every aspect of our daily lives is influenced by gov-ernmental policy and laws. All of that matters to Christians and most Americans. To what point can, or should, the government dictate what "we the people" should, do, think, or act? How is it, that a select group of leaders, rule over how we regulate our fam-ily values and beliefs? How can our elected leaders cower to the arm-twisting tactics of radical anti-life, anti-family groups like Black Lives Matter or Antifa?

It is possible and happening because we are not standing up and getting our votes cast. We are not joining with other people and groups to support candidates with sound values. If we don't like the laws, we need to elect leaders that hold to more sound principles. If we don't stand for our values and the constitution, all of rights and freedoms will be gone.

THE FINAL STRAW

The end game is this: a democrat controlled Washington, forever. The new democrat platform values government-sponsored, government-influenced, government control, of every aspect of American life, including reproduction and what a woman can or can not do with her own body. In other words, a socialist America. No rights, no guns, limited speech, regulations and restrictions, and individual liberty is dead. This is real and starting to happen. Look around, get informed, this is the final straw before the chaos turns into civil war.

The current democrat party is wrought with socialistic ideals of government dependence and power over the masses. The Kennedy-era Democrats are gone, or who are left in the party, are dead silent. There are moderate and conservative democrats. There are many good and decent Democrats who are pro-life. Does anyone ever hear a peep from them? Their party won't allow them to voice any dissenting opinion, and the fake news media never mentions anything of them. Those good honorable people are puppets of the radical left wing of the party. Do we want the radicals to regain power in Washington DC or your local government? "Kiss your rights goodbye."

Again, recall the Obama/Biden era. Eight years of governmental regulations, weak and decimated economic freefall, increasing taxes that drained your hard-earned resources, government failure to provide the promised health care, weak and disrespected influence worldwide, and division between the diverse peoples that make up America. What did they do for illegal aliens and our gun laws? Remember how the democrat leadership was anti-

Christian, anti-Israel? Look at the Johnson Law (if that's correct) where a pastor could not speak out about politics or politicians in the pulpit. Wasn't that a violation of our 1st Amendment rights? Exactly as mentioned earlier, but it was in fact happening. The Obama/Biden era, was a leftist, near socialistic government coupe that was moving to void every right and freedom we are suppose to have. This is just a foreshadow of the things to come, if we the people don't get active and elect good leaders.

Compare then to now. Are you better off with a Trump administration? More jobs, more in your paycheck, less government in your face, and a safer country. Have these last few years been better or worse for you and your family? Vote for whom benefits you best.

Rather than assess or describe a candidate, look at their records of how they have handled the affairs of the people. How do each of the democrats (and republicans); deal with the economy and taxes, national sovereignty, and protection of the citizens. How well did each handle health care, education, immigration and borders, protecting the rights and freedoms guaranteed under the Constitution? What was or is their stance in regards to guns, the constitution, church, life, and abortion? Of those principles that you value, how did each of these candidates fare? These are questions that should be asked at every election, for every candidate, regardless of party affiliation.

The Clinton era started this country on a downward spiral of the democrat party. With each successive candidate and leader, the party platform, their principles have moved further and further away from mainstream democrats, and most Americans. With every scandal, corruption, and dirty laundry exposed, it has turned away the masses of would-be democrat supporters; hence they supported Trump in 2016. Certainly, this may be greatly generalized, but to the average voter, Christian, republican, conservative, or other, the democrat party has greatly changed, and not for the better.

Voters can be swayed and convinced by the barrage of media propaganda and candidate promises. The Kennedy-era generation is gone. Now the Millennials, the Generation-X, the younger voters, are easily bamboozled by social media hype and fake biased news. The younger voter blocks are influenced by less than traditional values, and educational indoctrination by social activist teachers. Are they moved by candidate policies or promises? Perhaps they are more interested in the "feelings" and superficial things like the promises for free education, free health care, and free money, that gets their attention. "Kudos" to the democrat party voter outreach programs, it has been very successful in mass marketing. They reach out and follow up on interested voter prospects far better than any republican machine.

And the republican base is getting old. The ol' reliable republican base is changing, getting beyond voting age or ability, with poor outreach to the younger generation or the new citizen bases. The republican public image is that of old tired white men, supported by big business, along with being "racists". Family values and tradition doesn't register with the younger voters, especially as the decline in marital commitments continues to plummet, leaving disenfranchised families. The younger generations are more tolerant of anything other than restrictive Christian churchy dogma. And a biased media deflates any positives that republican leaders make, and exonerates the new democrat values over truth and impartiality.

WHAT TYPE OF LEADERS?

Who we elect, will result in laws by lawmakers, like those in New York, Vermont, and Virginia. The 2018 mid-term elections were wrought with manipulation and deceit, with the backing of main stream media, and powerful wealthy donors. The democrats were using Gestapo-like tactics to quell any resistance, twisting the truths and news, and used the "mob" to intimidate and harass opposition. This is not the Democrat Party of JFK or even Bill Clinton. What was the welfare of the working man under the Kennedy era Democrats, which was the cornerstone of the party, has given way to radical socialistic doctrine, with legions of brain-washed stooges to carry out mob violence and endless protests.

Rather than come up with solutions to fix an issue, or to make lives better for the people, they use rhetoric and hate speech, and the double standard to advance a dark agenda. That had in fact prompted the newly elected house legislatures in New York, Vermont, and Virginia, to design and pass such horrid abortion laws. Hey, as noted, elections have consequences, and if people don't get out there to vote, this is what happens. And what about your guns? Gone. They are coming for your private property, that is a fact.

Again, as an example, President Trump and the border wall. The will of the people that elected Trump, wanted a border wall and increased national security. It is fact that large amounts of drugs, crime, slavery, and masses of invading people, come across the southern border, nearly unchecked. Most Americans want this invasion to end. America is a sovereign nation that has the right to have a border, and restrict people and activities from entering the country. This is also factual, and mandated in the US Constitution that the president has the right and authority to protect and enforce our national borders from outside influences.

Bill Clinton argued and demanded a wall for protection along the border. So did Obama. Pelosi, Schumer, Ms. Clinton, and many other democrats, as shown on numerous video clips. Each cited the needs for border walls and security. Yet, because Trump is so greatly hated by most of the democrat leadership, the media, and their brainwashed masses, they all now oppose border security. For President Trump to succeed on this key election issue, the democrats would suffer greatly. Therefore, despite protecting Americans, our rights, our safety, the democrats have opposed every action President Trump has taken.

On and on, there seems to be examples of prominent party leaders that profess one thing, yet do the opposite. Too many of them make promises, only to deny such upon gaining office. Look at every major city, the promises made by the politicians, the billions of tax payer dollars, but no action. Granted, politics is an ugly business sometimes, and some candidates and elected people are morally corrupt, but that seems to be normal in this day and time in which we live. The latest opinion polls suggests that President Trump has an approval rating of about 50 to 55%, and Congress about 12 to 14%. Whether accurate or not, the fact is that many people don't trust or like our elected leaders. Then vote them out! Learn about the candidates before they get into office, and join with those that are like-minded. Use your rights and freedoms to assemble, speak up, and then vote.

The Nazis were a great lesson in socialism and the brainwashing of the people. They were socialists with a national theme (fascists). They came to power in a time of crisis, offering promises and protection. "The more you help us fix and change the laws, the more we can provide for your needs". Laws changed, power consolidated, to the point where the private ownership of guns was banned. Guns for personal protection were outlawed and taken from the people. Without the ability to protect yourself or stand against unjust rulers, freedoms of speech and religious practices were taken away from the people. More and more rights and freedoms were given up or taken away, to the point where Hitler became all powerful, pushing his personal agenda onto the nation and the world. How did that turn out for their citizens? How many millions, of their own citizens, did the government slaughter? Remember World War II, it was the result of corrupt leaders in power? Is the war still taught in our school system, or was it removed because it might offend somebody?

Along the same progression and results, the Russians under Stalin murdered millions and millions of their own citizens who opposed his gain of power. It was the same scenario as with Nazi Germany. A nation of laws, rights, and liberties, whittled away by leaders, then consolidating their power as given (or taken), to the death of the people, and ruin of the nation. Remember the tolerant society of the Soviet Union?

Not much is ever talked about Cambodia. Paul Pott, and the "Hitler youth-like Red Shirts", enforcing the dictates of the evil leadership, to the death of millions of peaceful citizens. Recall the grim stories of the killing fields? In every country, throughout Africa, South America, and Asia, where power is allowed to concentrate into the hands of a few rulers, abuse, oppression, and death follows. Every time, without fail, just study history. That is, if the history books are not re-written or burned to hide the truth. Beware, because history has a nasty way of repeating itself to the unwary.

The notion that socialism is "okay" or even good for a nation is absurd. It does not work, never has, never will. It can not, because "power corrupts, and absolute power corrupts absolutely". It has turned out disastrously for every nation since the dawn of man, and no rational way it can ever change. Human nature is that of violence and a thirst for power.

And when there is no longer in morale compass that is religiously based, then morality that is right or wrong, becomes based on "Human Relativism". There is no right, no wrong, everybody is free to think what they want. "My reality and what I believe is right or wrong, is different than your reality." Well, when the government says, that its ok to kill babies coming out of the birth canal, and that it's the right of the mother and her doctors, then that is a country nearing total destruction. Then it will be, that the lawyers and leaders will make the laws to justify killing older children, the elderly, and "those racist Christians always pushing their morality, it hurts my feelings". Our babies are being slaughtered today, and the Christians will be persecuted tomorrow. Who would have ever guessed that America would sink so low?

The difference with now, and our governmental structure, is God. America was founded with a Judeo-Christian belief, becoming the foundational stones of every law and thought written in the US Constitution. The leftists and educational elitists will deny that, and scream about some insane alternate reality, but fact is fact. They are working diligently to change the books and the facts, to hide these truths. If libraries still exist where books (the kind with ink and paper) still reside, one can research the writings of every founding father and framer of the document to read of their faith-based ideology. Is that a bad thing? The leftists of the democrat party would say so, because their agenda is very different.

America has lasted for over two hundred years, with the ideas that individuals are good if not oppressed by their rulers, and that man can do good works. Look at what America has done, created, built, fought for, stood against, the freedoms and liberties enjoyed, and so on. There are a lot of negative things that has happened over this time also. True, but the system of this government, for people to rise up and make positive changes for all, has prevailed. The American system of government, built on our religious premise, has worked for the health and happiness of all (or most anyways). The American system of representative government is not perfect. We are flawed people, and sometimes we mess up. We can be greedy, hateful, self-servicing, and so on, but the government was designed to balance the concentration of powers, which has worked well until recently.

Our system of government, guarantees the rights and privileges of the individual is protected. We have the freedom to speak out against the government, and someone who wails against the goodness of our country, is also protected. Why change this? Why would any rational sober person think there is a better system to govern a nation? Apparently, there many, and organizations that see it differently. Perhaps we can still avoid the coming civil war.

A COUPLE FINAL THOUGHTS

Remember what Machiavelli said back around 1500, "Power corrupts, and absolute power corrupts absolutely". And examining history, even recent history, this is exactly true. When leaders get into power, unchecked by laws and constitutional limitations, then the mischief that resides in a mans' heart, festers into evil. Power is a drug, and intoxication that drives leaders mad, and brings ruin to nations. The victims are the citizens.

It is said that if a government is allowed to gain power (unchecked), then those leaders first abuse the power to their own gain. Then they oppress the people and silence opposition. And then, by historical fact, they mass murder their citizens. And it starts with the babies.

If democrat politicians (who have the mission to control the lives of the people) are elected, they will enact laws to reduce or eliminate the rights and privileges we hold. In particular, our rights to bear arms, the freedom to worship God as we like, the ability speak in opposition of the government or laws that are enacted, our rights to join together in public or private, are all gravely at risk. As we lose our freedom of speech (again as an example), we become slaves to the government. Power and control unchecked, will destroy a nation. Killing the most innocent and precious of God's creation, our babies, He will repay in kind, and destroy this nation. God will not be mocked, even if cleverly worded by a legal document.

Our system of government was designed and set up to assure the people would have the liberty to become all they can aspire to do (if not murdered at birth). The freedom of free and open speech, and religious liberties, have been the cornerstone of this country, rooted in the process of free and open elections. Every vote counts, and every citizen has a duty to make this country better, according to their own conscience.

As our society writhes with turmoil, the next election cycle approaches. Many groups are seeking to undermine our rights and liberties to vote, to own and carry firearms, to have free and open speech, our rights to worship, and the rights afforded to life. It is critical for the survival of the nation as a whole; to learn about the candidates and what they value, and stand with those who values the things you value. This is no time for professing Christians, or any American to sit idle, there is just too much at stake.

This little story is critically important to keep in mind.

"A bunch of sheep were happily grazing in the field, enjoying the comforts of their lives. A wolf came out of the woods and killed one of the sheep. In a panic, they formed a consensus on what to do. They decided the best way to keep themselves safe was to remove all of their teeth. Later, the wolf came back and killed them all."

Set that clearly in your mind. Laws only work if they are enforced, and, if everyone follows them. Those who are unlawful, and there are too many in America, do not follow the laws. Be wary of the politicians.

And lastly, keep in mind what Gods word tells us: "Repent, and turn away from what we are doing". There are many scriptures that continually repeat this, like Zechariah 1:3 and 4, in part reads, "...Thus says the Lord of hosts, 'Return to Me' declares the Lord of Hosts." "...Return now from your evil ways and from your evil deeds". Not to do so, invites the wrath that is coming to this country. May the Lord be with you, and all of us.

AND WHAT TO DO?

America is at a crossroad; it's a time of strife and division among two major lines of thinking. One side is trying to uphold and live by the traditional values and framework of the country, namely the Constitution.

The other side is trying to tear down every positive thing in America because "it's unfair", "racist", "full of greedy rich white men", "the republicans don't care about the planet", and every other nonsense imaginable. They are the ones that are pushing for a government all-powerful solution to solve all the nations ills, more control, "equality and fairness for all", confiscate the guns, and everyone will live happily ever-after in a unicorn-filled safe la-la land. As Nancy Pelosi, Speaker of the House, irrationally screams, "why does anyone need more than one gun? The answer is simply, "because of socialist nut-jobs like her".

Buy more guns, stock up on ammo, train, and join like-minded organizations that support your values. Vote. Vote, and encourage everyone you meet to vote as well. Your vote is your voice, the correct way to make the peaceful change in leadership. Also, learn, research the topics of the day and decide for yourself, which is true, and what is biased agenda-driven rhetoric. Study about our history, and make sure your children or grandkids learn our true history also.

Also consider prayer. Get into a pure and good prayerful time with your God, and beg for mercy and forgiveness. Repent of whatever darkness holds you down, and ask for His help and grace to change your heart. Then give Him praise before you do anything more. Give praise upon the Lord, then pray for your enemies. Prayers that our leaders making and supporting these evil laws, and the organizations and people also supporting such, have a change of heart. After praying for our enemies, pray for America. Prayers should include for wisdom, guidance, and repentant hearts. Prayers for our "good" leaders, organizations, and others that hold sound doctrine and values. Pray, lots of prayer, that is our best and easiest weapon to wield.

Why pray? "We need action! We need to do this, or do that." Yes, perhaps true, but this is not really our fight, it's Gods. We are Gods hands and feet, His voice and light in this dark world. But first we need to pray. Because there is Power in prayer, power by invoking the name of Jesus, and it is through His Spirit, in the spiritual realm, that the real work gets done. Then, go out and do something to share the love of God.

Positive changes will come, and perhaps we can avoid the Second American Civil War.

ABOUT THE AUTHOR

I grew up in a middle class family, had a father that worked, a mother that stayed home and raised children, the typical traditional American home. We had a small house, one car, (no) white picket fence, we had pets, guns, regular schooling, church-goers, watched news and various TV shows, hunted and shot targets, and had all of the cliche normal things in life typified during the 1950s and 60s. Life was normal and decent, reasonably peaceful, and safe.

My father was a veteran, worked a blue collar job, and was a straight-line democrat, just like his father before him. The Kennedy era thinking of party politics was pretty much his thinking as well. And for many decades, that seemed to work well in America. I too learned and adopted similar ideas of how life and government should work and coexist.

But that has changed radically over the past couple decades, as the democrat party is no longer the party of the average working man. One would best describe the party as what we used to call the Communist-Socialist party during that earlier era. Now the party is all about hate speech, bigotry, division, dirty-politics, rampant dishonesty and deception by party leaders and candidates, and everything revolving around government control. This is no longer the democrat party America once loved.

The candidates and false narratives they promoted were enough to make me switch to the Republican Party. Over the last many election cycles while the democrats drove further left, I pushed my family and friends to switch parties and vote further right.

Not that the republicans are perfect by any means, but they do hold to more of the values and principles I do. The biggest area where they align with my own thinking are the ideas of limited government, the sanctity of life, and support for the Constitution. Upholding our rights and freedoms are more their forte, so this is where we will stay.

My hope is to share these thoughts with you, so that you can glean some insight of the struggle we face over our dying liberties. Thank you reading this.

Also consider these other books written about our Rights and Freedoms. These also are found on Amazon Kindle under the Politics section. Look for:

"The Democrat Blue Wave is the Zombie Apocalypse"
by T. H. Logwood
ASIN: B07MYBFKT1

* * * * *

Don't Tread on Me
By T. H. Logwood
ASIN: B07X5DRRYB

* * * * *

I Met a Man Named Donald
By T. H. Logwood
ASIN: B0842YF1HH.

* * * * *

"The End of American Liberty"
by T. H. Logwood
ASIN: B07HPYZWTF

* * * * *

Repent America, In the Name of Jesus!
By T. H. Logwood
ASIN: B07NBXYLLB

* * * * *

The Democrat Blue Wave is the Texas 2nd Alamo
By T. H. Logwood
ASIN: B07N7N2WG6

* * * * *

"The End of American Freedom"
by T. H. Logwood
ASIN: B07MSJ4QD7

* * * * *

"The U.S.S. La Porte (APA 151), The Pearl of the Pacific"
by T. H. Logwood
ASIN: B07L6JXRB9